African Writers Talking
▼▼▼▼▼▼▼▼▼▼▼▼▼▼▼▼▼▼▼▼▼▼▼▼▼▼▼▼▼▼▼

Among the books written and discussed by
the authors interviewed in *African Writers Talking*,
the following are published by AFRICANA:

Wole Soyinka
The Interpreters

Christopher Okigbo
Labyrinths with 'Path of Thunder'

Mazisi Kunene
Zulu Poems

John Pepper Clark
America, Their America
Casualties, Poems 1966/68

African Writers Talking
▼▼▼▼▼▼▼▼▼▼▼▼▼▼▼▼▼▼▼▼▼▼▼▼

*A collection of
radio interviews*

Edited by
COSMO PIETERSE & DENNIS DUERDEN

 AFRICANA PUBLISHING CORPORATION
NEW YORK

Published
in the United States of America 1972
by Africana Publishing Corporation
101 Fifth Avenue
New York, NY 10003

© Dennis Duerden and Cosmo Pieterse 1972
in selection and editorial matter
First published 1972
All rights reserved

Library of Congress Catalog Card No. 72-75255
ISBN 0-8419-0118-X (cloth)
0-8419-0119-8 (paper)

Printed in Great Britain

Contents

▼▼▼▼▼▼▼▼▼▼▼▼▼▼▼▼▼▼▼▼▼▼▼▼

Introduction		vii
CHINUA ACHEBE	*interviewed by Lewis Nkosi*	3
	interviewed by Donatus Nwoga	6
	interviewed by Dennis Duerden	9
	interviewed by Robert Serumaga	11
AMA ATA AIDOO	*interviewed by Maxine McGregor*	19
KOFI AWOONOR	*interviewed by Robert Serumaga*	29
	interviewed by Dennis Duerden	37
DENNIS BRUTUS	*interviewed by Cosmo Pieterse*	53
J. P. CLARK	*interviewed by Lewis Nkosi*	63
	interviewed by Andrew Salkey	68
	interviewed by Andrew Salkey	71
CYPRIAN EKWENSI	*interviewed by Lewis Nkosi*	77
	interviewed by Dennis Duerden	80
MAZISI KUNENE	*interviewed by Lewis Nkosi*	85
	interviewed by Alex La Guma	88
ALEX LA GUMA	*interviewed by Robert Serumaga*	91
EZEKIEL MPHAHLELE	*interviewed by Dennis Duerden*	95
	interviewed by Robert Serumaga	98
	interviewed by Cosmo Pieterse	101
JOHN NAGENDA	*interviewed by Lewis Nkosi*	115
	interviewed by Robert Serumaga	117

NGUGI WA THIONG'O	*interviewed by Dennis Duerden*	121
	interviewed by Aminu Abdullahi	124
CHRISTOPHER OKIGBO	*interviewed by Lewis Nkosi*	133
	interviewed by Dennis Duerden	139
	interviewed by Robert Serumaga	143
OKOT P'BITEK	*interviewed by Robert Serumaga*	149
RICHARD RIVE	*interviewed by Lewis Nkosi*	157
	interviewed by Robert Serumaga	159
WOLE SOYINKA	*interviewed by Ezekiel Mphahlele*	169
	interviewed by Lewis Nkosi	171
	interviewed by Dennis Duerden	178
EFUA SUTHERLAND	*interviewed by Maxine Lautré*	183

Introduction

▼▼▼▼▼▼▼▼▼▼▼▼▼▼▼▼▼▼▼▼▼▼▼▼▼▼▼▼▼▼

THIS COLLECTION of interviews comes from a sizeable library of discussions, talks and interviews that the Transcription Centre amassed over a period of some six years. The Transcription Centre, whose Director is Dennis Duerden, originally produced tapes of these interviews for broadcasting over various radio networks in Africa. Hitherto these interviews have been confined to the limited and immediate radio audiences for which each was initially intended. That the interviews should become available to a reading public is something long looked forward to by many of us who have seen transcriptions of the tapes and have read excerpts of the interviews printed in *Cultural Events in Africa*. These interviews represent an important aspect of the work of the Transcription Centre.

They help us in a stock-taking of the writers. Across the continent readers ask questions about Achebe, Aidoo, Awoonor, Brutus, Clark and Ekwensi. How do they write? Why do they write about particular things? How do they feel about such topics as negritude, commitment and the writer as teacher? These are some of the questions that these interviews seek to answer.

These recurring themes indicate the importance of meeting the writer as a person as well as an author. Authors in Africa today often write from a strongly felt social position that is akin to the position of the dedicated prophet. For him or her it is often the large social themes or questions or problems that are to be dealt with, not only as citizen or politician, but also as poet, playwright or novelist. And it is for this reason that the enduring question of 'Why do you write about these matters?' is asked so often and so insistently by interviewers.

These interviews fit in with the overall outlines of African literary endeavour in English between 1962 and 1969. There is an attempt to define 'African Literature'. The kind of questions asked in these interviews, as indeed in the conferences of the period, are 'What is African writing?', 'What is an African style, theme, diction, audience?' They link themselves to answers that relate to negritude and neo-Africanism, to linguistic, geographical and ethnic considerations. Stimulated by social and political events, the two major literary themes are colonialism (the culture clash, exposure of exploitation and pre-independence dehumanization, the struggle for liberation) and Arcadia (pre-colonial past, the social and ethical norms of traditional African society, the old Empires). This was at a time when most new African authors had been published sparsely: the occasional volume and an appearance in various magazines such as *Black Orpheus*, *The New African*, *Transition* and *Africa South*.

Between 1964 and 1966 a shift in emphasis was taking place. Instead of the relatively theoretical debates on a definition of African literature, we begin to hear more realistic discussion. Now academics and authors, critics and creators ask for a place to be given to African writing in the study of literature in African universities. There is a growth of research into traditional oral literature. There is more translation. So African vernacular and African literature in European languages are made more widely accessible and interact with one another.

The two earlier themes of colonialism and Arcadia have given way to a more urgent scrutiny of the here and now. A satirical eye becomes focused on the modern free and venal states in Africa and authors talk about commitment. They talk out their commitment to political and social ideas and ideals to the extent in some cases of courting exile, imprisonment and artistic silence.

Side by side with this public stand and the tone of voice that is employed for its purposes, a new privacy of tone develops too. And in this phase, the third stage in an African literature that is scarcely a generation old, a new critical awareness has been brought to bear on a literature that may have been forced to sprint before it could walk. Thus a new aesthetic is being developed out of the socio-economic and political, as well as cultural and ideological, pressures of the new free African states.

Lewis Nkosi and Robert Serumaga have handled many of these interviews. Partly as a result of this the interviews presented in this volume are mainly of two types. The Nkosi interviews of 1962/1963 usually follow what one might call a literary formula: Lewis Nkosi asks for biographical background, and about literary influences and finds out about future projects. This kind of interview has the advantage of filling in part of the literary and personal background to the writer and may assist the reader in his own analysis and enjoyment of that author. If a reader knows that a writer likes or has been influenced by a particular school or movement or individual, or that he has been brought up in such and such a manner, in such and such a place, he may find new interest in the style of writing and the development and exploration of the themes by the writer; he may find a relationship between fictional incidents and the events of a writer's life. Some may argue that this is not the business of literary criticism;

Introduction ix

Robert Serumaga   *Lewis Nkosi*

others will find much of value which helps their critical assessment of a writer.

The Serumaga type of interview assumes that the audience already has considerable knowledge. He also assumes that this audience requires as far as is possible a frank and direct confession of some of the innermost and most complex parts of the writer's conscious personal life, philosophy and working methods, especially in so far as these concern the relationship between himself and his beliefs and the heroes, situations and structure of his works.

My own contact with these interviews goes back to 1965 when I first used to go to the Transcription Centre and meet some of the writers in its rooms and studios. My knowledge of African literature was strengthened by listening to these interviews as they were made, as well as participating in some of them.

My own experience has convinced me of the uniqueness of the Transcription Centre's collection of tape-recorded interviews. It is an archive of great historical interest, giving an essential first-hand account of the development of post-Independence African literature. For this period the Transcription Centre's records and accounts are admirably full, including critics, poets, novelists, dramatists, artists and editors from East, West, Central and Southern Africa. They are interviewed on their own work, their creative resources and sources, their influences, on their aims and projects, and on their research within a framework that relates them constantly to the African audience.   Cosmo Pieterse

Acknowledgements

Acknowledgement is made to the following for photographs of authors and interviewers:

Chinua Achebe – Lotte Meitner-Graf, London
Ama Ata Aidoo and Cyprian Ekwensi – John Goldblatt, London
Kofi Awoonor – Sandra Gatten, New York
J. P. Clark and Lewis Nkosi – The Transcription Centre
Mazisi Kunene, Okot p'Bitek and Robert Serumaga – Valerie Wilmer, London
Alex La Guma – *Horizon Magazine*, Zambia
Ezekiel Mphahlele – Clive Bubley, London
John Nagenda and Wole Soyinka – Marilyn Stafford
Ngugi wa Thiong'o – East African Newspapers, Nairobi
Christopher Okigbo – *Nigeria Magazine*
Richard Rive – Messrs. Faber & Faber, London.

African Writers Talking

Chinua Achebe
BORN 1930

▼▼▼▼▼▼▼▼▼▼▼▼▼▼▼▼▼▼▼▼▼▼▼▼▼▼▼▼▼▼▼

Interviewed by Lewis Nkosi in Lagos, August 1962. At the time of recording this interview Chinua Achebe was Director of the External Service of the Nigerian Broadcasting Corporation. He had already published with Heinemann *Things Fall Apart* (1958) and *No Longer at Ease* (1960), and was working on *Arrow of God* which was published in 1964. A fourth novel *A Man of the People* (1966) was to be followed by the publication of his short stories under the title *Girls at War, and other stories* (Heinemann 1972). Achebe has published some children's books, as well as *The Sacrificial Egg, and other stories* (Etudo, Onitsha 1962).
Chinua Achebe was educated at Government College, Umuahia, and at University College, Ibadan, where he was one of the first graduates to take a full degree course. In 1954 he joined the Nigerian Broadcasting Corporation, and was Director of External Broadcasting until 1966. His first two novels – *Things Fall Apart* (1958) and *No Longer at Ease* (1960) – have been published in many countries; *Arrow of God* (1964) was awarded the first Jock Campbell/*New Statesman* Award; and *A Man of the People* aroused widespread interest on its first publication in January 1966. In 1970 he became a Senior Research Fellow in the Institute of African Studies at Nsukka.

NKOSI   Well, Chinua Achebe, you are one of the leading novelists in Nigeria, you're famous in America, and England, as well as Europe. When did you really begin to write?

ACHEBE   I wrote *Things Fall Apart* in 1958, or rather it was published in '58 – I started work on it around '56 – towards the end of '56. But the story itself had been sort of maturing in my mind for about two years previously.

NKOSI   When did you really become interested in writing as an art, something that you might use throughout your life? Did you start this at school?

ACHEBE   Well, I think at the university at Ibadan, I can't say definitely when it was but I know around '51, '52, I was quite certain that I was going to try my hand at writing, and one of the things that set me thinking was Joyce Carey's novel set in Nigeria, *Mr Johnson,* which was praised so much, and it was clear to me that this was a most superficial picture of – not only of the country, but even of the Nigerian character and so I thought if this was famous, then perhaps someone ought to try and look at this from the inside.

NKOSI   Yes; well, according to the blurb in one of your books, you had been sent to the university to study medicine, is that correct?

ACHEBE   Yes, that's right, it's just one of those things: you see, when I left school I didn't really know what I wanted to do and medicine was very glamorous – it was either medicine or engineering – but I soon discovered that it wasn't really my cup of tea, so I changed.

NKOSI   Of the two books you have written, which gives you the greatest satisfaction?

ACHEBE   That's very difficult – it's really quite impossible to say, it depends on when I am asked this question: some days I feel happier with *Things Fall Apart,* some days with the other one. They are so different, you see; I think it's rather like one's children, perhaps – you know, you like one for certain things and the other for other things. *Things Fall Apart* I wrote with more affection, but that doesn't mean I prefer it, I wrestled a lot more with *No Longer At Ease,* and so I think that probably, *No Longer at Ease* is better, technically, but that's as far as I can go.

NKOSI   Yes; well, most of us would probably differ with the author himself since lots of us like the first one very much; the texture of the writing seems to be so much more finished and syntactically finished. What are you working on at the moment?

ACHEBE   I'm trying to, you see, what I've decided to do really is to oscillate between the past – the immediate past – and the present: *Things Fall Apart* is about a hundred years ago; *No Longer at Ease* is today; and I want to go back now to not quite the time of *Things Fall Apart,* but a little later, because I think there's a lot of interesting material there; and the fourth one would be present day. And that's the way I intend to work.

NKOSI   There is quite a community of writers in Nigeria. Could you tell us something about this, whether there is any social intercourse between you and the younger writers writing at the moment or do you lead an isolated life?

ACHEBE   Well, you see there are so few – that's the thing, so it's quite easy to get to know one another and I think most of the younger writers have been students at the University College, Ibadan – so it's a community.

In Lagos here we are trying to start a writers' club, well, a society of authors really, but it's not so that we can get acquainted but to have a platform, you know, to do battle if necessary.

NKOSI   Yes; now, as a professional broadcaster do you find much time to do your own writing, and what hours do you use for writing?

ACHEBE   Well, I find that if I have a story that I badly want to tell I can always find the time. Of course, it is becoming increasingly difficult for me to write as quickly as I would want. The novel on which I am working now is taking me much longer than I had thought. But it doesn't matter: I don't think the speed is all that important.

NKOSI   Is this latest novel that you are working on centred around Lagos or does it deal with the urban community?

ACHEBE   No, it goes back to the village. You see, it goes back to what I've said before: if I want to write about Nigeria, say a hundred years ago, seventy-five years ago, it has to be the village society. The present day would be Lagos and the towns.

NKOSI   Yes. It is very interesting how well you are able to capture the nuances of tribal life. Have you lived in the rural areas yourself?

ACHEBE   Yes. I was brought up in a village, went to school there; I didn't really get into any big town until I went to Ibadan, and you see, in the villages in Nigeria – well where I come from in the Eastern Region, life is still – well things are changing very fast but if one is interested, one can still see signs of what life used to look like.

NKOSI   Do you yourself find this ambivalent? Did you, at the time when you were growing up, have the feeling that you were no longer at ease with the rural scene and at the same time find that you had a tremendous affection for the life of your people in the rural setting. How did you reconcile this within yourself?

ACHEBE   Well, as a little boy it didn't worry me at all. I took most of these things for granted. I was born into a Christian family, you see my father was a missionary and that was the life of the . . . You know, the sort of civilized life of the village was us, but it was only later – even though I was brought up as a Christian, the life of the village was there for you to see – it was only later that I began to evaluate, so to speak.

NKOSI   Yes. Were you overseas very long?

ACHEBE   No, I've only been out once to Britain in '56 for a short period at the BBC.

NKOSI   What would you say are the main influences on your life, say, from the point of view of literature? Whom do you admire most amongst writers?

ACHEBE   That again is very difficult. I don't really think that there's any one I can say I admire all that much. I used to like Hemingway; and I used to like Conrad, I used to like Conrad particularly; and I like Graham Greene, I find him a bit heavy going now and again but I do like him; and some of the younger people like Kingsley Amis and – well, I don't have any special favourites.

NKOSI   Now, if we may just ask this rather peculiar question, just how much power does a professional artist, a professional writer, have in a society like Lagos or the Nigerian society as a whole?

ACHEBE   Not much, because writing is so new and we are only just beginning to be known but I think by power you don't mean –

NKOSI   I mean influence.

ACHEBE   Influence, yes, well I think that will come; if one writes good novels or writes good poetry, he's bound to have an influence but I don't see much of it at present, only the beginnings, you see, in the schools and that sort of thing, which shows that perhaps the next generation will be influenced by what we write today.

NKOSI   Yes. Do you set yourself any particular time schedule for your writing: how many novels, for instance, you have to do within a year, you know, that sort of thing?

ACHEBE   No, no, I don't; you see, I think writing is such a serious thing that one ought to take it fairly easily and slowly, you know, at its own pace. I don't like forcing a story. Some days, weeks even, I can't write anything, and I don't want to go to the table and start scribbling, you see, I feel it's – it is an important thing and ought to be taken seriously.

This interview was recorded in the year that Chinua Achebe published *Arrow of God*. The interview, with Donatus Nwoga, took place during the Conference on Commonwealth Literature, held at Leeds University in September 1964.

NWOGA   I was fortunate to listen to Mr Achebe address the Conference on Commonwealth Literature recently and he made certain statements about the duty of the author, or the responsibilities of the author, which, I suppose, you could also accept as a privilege in a developing society. I wonder, Mr Achebe, would you indicate what you think is the duty, the privilege, the responsibility of the author, in the situation in which you find yourself?

ACHEBE   Well, what I was trying to get at is this – it's difficult to put in a very few words, but what I wanted to put across was this: that we writers in – say a writer like myself in Nigeria – should not take for granted the relationships which exist between writers and their audience in another society, like, say, Britain; because we tend to do this and I think we might be neglecting our proper function if we take anything for granted instead of thinking what exactly is our society, what are its needs, what can I do, what can I contribute; this is what I was trying to get at, and I think we have a very important function. In this paper I saw my role, this is only one of the roles of the writer, as a teacher.

NWOGA As a teacher, this of course differentiates the purpose of literature in societies which have been so well established that literature is an exercise of those who have the time for it, and a society like ours where people don't read so much that they can afford to waste the time they spend in reading. They tend to think of literature as a source of some sort of education, some sort of learning.

ACHEBE I was using teacher there, not in the narrow sense of teaching a scale or teaching to pass an examination. I was thinking primarily more of a deeper meaning of teaching and what I had in mind, what I think a novelist can teach is something very fundamental, namely to indicate to his readers, to put it crudely, that we in Africa did not hear of culture for the first time from Europeans.

NWOGA I wonder, instead of making a long comment myself, whether you could repeat some of the stories I've heard you tell of letters you got from people who have enjoyed your stories?

ACHEBE Well, I think I'll give two or three illustrations. One was from Northern Nigeria, which I was very pleased to get, because one doesn't usually get reaction from that part. This was a letter from someone who had just left school, and he said something like, 'I don't usually write to writers, no matter how good their work is or how interesting, but I thought I should write to you because you, I think, you teach us young people a lot, you see, and I hope you will carry on teaching us.' Now this is one of them, and then there was the other one, which was rather pathetic, from a student in Ghana who said I had neglected to include questions and answers at the end of *Things Fall Apart*, and could I rectify this position so that he would pass his school certificate next year.

NWOGA You mentioned earlier that you wanted to tell the people that we didn't first hear about culture when the Europeans came. I wonder whether you could develop this a bit?

ACHEBE Yes, what I think is the basic problem of a new African country like Nigeria is really what you might call a 'crisis in the soul'. We have been subjected – we have subjected ourselves too – to this period during which we have accepted everything alien as good and practically everything local or native as inferior. I could give you illustrations of when I was growing up, the attitude of our parents, the Christian parents, to Nigerian dances, to Nigerian handicrafts; and the whole society during this period began to look down on itself, you see, and this was a very bad thing; and we haven't actually, even now with the independence, we still haven't got over this period. I can give again the example of the boy in my wife's class who said he wouldn't write about the harmattan because it was 'bush', you see: he would rather write about winter. Now things like this show one that the writer has the responsibility to teach his audience that there is nothing shameful about the harmattan, that it is not only daffodils that can make a fit subject for poetry, but the palm tree and so on. This is what I was getting at.

NWOGA   You have even pointed this out in your novel *No Longer At Ease*; there is the politician, Honourable Sam Okoli, who keeps saying he once had a graduate from Ibadan who wouldn't call him 'Sir', but he was pleased he had as his secretary somebody who went to Cambridge, an English person, who was calling him 'Sir' and he appeared to be extremely excited about all this.

ACHEBE   Oh yes, yes I know the aspect of this whole complex, colonial complex which you cannot eradicate overnight. You see, a writer has a responsibility to try and stop this because unless our culture begins to take itself seriously it will never sort of get off the ground.

NWOGA   Yes. I remember one self-styled critic suggesting that you were opposing colonialism while at the same time enjoying the fruits of colonialism: living in Lagos, writing and all that. Do you think he was right in assessing you as being opposed to colonialism as such?

ACHEBE   Well, that is a very stupid comment. I mean, to oppose colonialism does not mean that one does not appreciate the values of Western technological civilization. I mean the two things don't come in as necessarily conflicting and such a comment should be beneath notice.

NWOGA   I thought so myself. There's another thing too I think I would like to mention: maybe I shouldn't say it's the same person, but it was the same person, who said something about your misunderstanding of African religion. He referred in particular to this word 'chi' which was translated as one's personal God and he thought that he had studied Ibo religion enough to indicate this wasn't a personal God, but the God within. Do you see any distinction between . . .

ACHEBE   I think the man was talking through his hat. I know who you are talking about now and I wouldn't normally spend any time discussing him but in this particular case I think he was completely wrong. I saw this article* and he was talking about 'chi' as the God with the capital G. I take it you are using the equivalent of the Christian God, perhaps God Almighty within. I mean this is complete balderdash, because trying to translate a word like 'chi' into English always carries its own problems. When I say 'personal God' it's not perfect but it's as close as I could get. Now I think the best translation would be 'personal spirit', not 'personal God', but 'God within' is just trash.

NWOGA   I thought so, because it rather felt like the imposition on the African of a certain Western, possibly Christian, metaphysics.

The next interview was recorded with Dennis Duerden talking to Chinua Achebe in Lagos, in September 1965.

DUERDEN   Chinua, one has the feeling after reading your novel *Things Fall Apart* that the contemporary Nigerian Society from which you spring must have preserved the patterns of African traditional life to a large degree, if not in the cities, at least in the villages. Is this true?

ACHEBE   Yes, I think it is true to a large extent; certainly it was true when I was growing up. I think it's not quite so true today because the change is sort of accelerating, but when I was growing up in my village, it was still possible to catch glimpses of what the complete traditional society must have looked like and one supplemented these impressions with accounts, stories told by old people – like my father. Now, my father, although he was a Christian convert, was very useful to me in this way because he told me how things were in the past. And I'd like to say, too, it's not only in the villages; even in the cities, if you look carefully enough, you can see patterns of the past too; it depends on how closely you look. If you take Lagos, for instance, today: you will find that many villages from the hinterland are presented here as units what you might call the improvement societies. Each village has its own meeting, perhaps the women have their dances and so on and the men hold some traditional celebrations and so on. So, the patterns although much paler today, the patterns are still there.

DUERDEN   Yes, when you wrote *Things Fall Apart* did you actually do it from a historical point of view, describing history, or was it from these experiences of yours when you were growing up?

ACHEBE   It was purely from the experience and of course a bit of

* Cf. *Transition*, Vol. 3, No. 13, Mar.–Apr. 1964, p. 36f. 'The Offended *Chi* in Achebe's Novels' by Austin J. Shelton. Nwoga's letter in reply, 'The *Chi* Offended' is in Vol. 4, No. 15, 1964, p. 5.

imagination. I didn't have to do any research as such. The festivals were still there, most of them were still there, the whole attitude, really it's the attitude of the people; their philosophy of life was still there. I mean, you could see it; and the rest really was using your own imagination to create the details of the story.

DUERDEN   What village actually did you live in?

ACHEBE   A place called Ogidi, which is six miles from the Niger.

DUERDEN   This was during the thirties, was it?

ACHEBE   That's right.

DUERDEN   I've heard that there was a big wave of Christian conversion in the thirties which destroyed a number of the traditional places and things which went on there. Like ritual plays. Is this true?

ACHEBE   Well, actually this may have been before the thirties because when I was growing up it was not very common to see people converted. I know we used to go out every fourth Sunday into the village, the Christians, I mean, and sing and preach and the pagans, as they were called, would assemble and listen; you see, the idea was that we could convert a few others. I don't remember that we met with any great success. In fact many of the people who turned up, were what you might call 'backsliders', some who had been in the Church and had given it up, and they put some rather embarrassing questions to the catechist or the pastor. So in all I think the peak of conversion was much earlier than the thirties.

DUERDEN   Yes. When I was in Ibadan I saw this film J. P. Clark has made about a play which takes place amongst his own people, the Ijaw, and it's about a seven day play which was performed about twenty or thirty years ago which hasn't been performed since, which he got them to revive. He got an old man who told the story, and he got local actors to do it. Do you know anything about it?

ACHEBE   Well I know J.P.'s play. In fact, I have read his, sort of, modern version of it, which is extremely good. I do not think we did have that kind of extended drama in my area, not as far as I know, but what I do remember were skits, you know, short skits performed by masks or masqueraders, usually at the expense of some members of the community, those who had fallen out of favour, rather short satirical pieces, but nothing of the extent of J.P.'s Ijaw play.

DUERDEN   They'd be like Egungun.*

ACHEBE   Yes.

DUERDEN   And these still exist, do they?

---

* Originally dancers wearing ancestral-spirit masks. Now masked dancer-actors who perform generally satirical episodes and poems; Western Nigerian. The masks worn are of social stereotypes.

ACHEBE Not really now, no. I think perhaps the only thing remaining is the night masquerades which were often very powerful in the past. You see, they came out at night and went from house to house, and sang, and also indulged in gossip, you see, again at the expense of anyone who was not toeing the line of the village. This is pure entertainment and this still happens, apart from masquerades at festivals, not only at traditional ones but at Christmas and Easter and so on: all this, the whole trend, is really towards a light-hearted version of our old entertainment.

DUERDEN What are the night masquerades? What were they called?

ACHEBE They were called Egwugwu and they were really beyond the law practically. They could sing what they liked, they went from A's house to B's house and they would say some nasty things about A in B's house, and then go to C and say some nasty things about B. Usually things based on fact, you see, but normally things people would not say in the daytime, and this was the way that – just for amusement.

When this interview was recorded with Chinua Achebe, his fourth novel *A Man of the People* had just been published. He had left his post as Director of External Service of the Nigerian Broadcasting Corporation in the same year, 1966.

The interview was conducted by Robert Serumaga in the studios of the Transcription Centre in London, in February 1967.

SERUMAGA Chinua, you were born in Nigeria at a place called Ogidi which is near Onitsha?

ACHEBE That's right.

SERUMAGA Now, when you were born I think Captain Lugard had been and gone and there had been changes brought about by the British invasion of Africa. How did you manage at that particular time to get so much insight into the kind of society, pre-colonial society you write about?

ACHEBE Well actually the pre-colonial society in Africa had not completely disappeared. I was brought up in a village and looking around you could see not the whole society, but you could see enough of what was left to be able to fill in the gaps. And if you were interested in the old Africa – as I was instinctively: I mean, this was something that came to me naturally, I just was interested – you could see it and you could ask questions.

SERUMAGA Did you have any specific kind of role in the society which would have given you advantages in gaining certain kinds of information about rituals and things like that?

ACHEBE   No, on the contrary I was almost excluded from it. On looking back, if I had any advantage, this was it: that my father had been a missionary, he was retired when I was growing up; and we were Christians and in our village you had two sides – the 'people of the Church', as we were called, and the 'people of the world', the others. And there was a certain amount of distance; although we were in the same village there was a certain distance, which I think made it possible for me not to take things for granted you see. I say this because as for some of the people who grew up with me, whose parents were heathen, as we called them, these things did not strike them. This is what they tell me today: they took things for granted. Whereas I went to church on Sunday, we prayed every morning and so on, and the rest of the village I could see from a slight distance.

SERUMAGA   Now this distance in your part of the country, did it produce any real conflict in the sense that, for example in James Ngugi's book *The River Between*, there is this kind of cultural conflict. Did it create any conflict between the heathen and the Christians?

ACHEBE   No, not really. I think they had come to co-exist quite peacefully, and the Church and the world co-existed. In the same family, an extended family, you had some members belonging to this side and some others to the other side; there was certainly no violent conflict at all.

SERUMAGA   What about the conflict of one's own character? The sort of person who'd grown up with parents in that kind of traditionally-based family, and then be Christianized at the same time? Did it happen on an individual basis that one experienced this conflict between one's belief and traditions?

ACHEBE   Yes, for me, it did. When I was growing up I didn't obviously think of it in those terms – I was merely curious. When there was a festival in the village we were supposed not to visit our neighbours because they were likely to give us food offered to idols. Now we always managed to visit – my sister and I – we were curious. And it was only later, when you came to think of it in terms of philosophy and so on, that you begin to react against this. But at that stage I was merely curious to see what was going on on the other side.

SERUMAGA   In at least two of your books you create situations where you have a character who has a son who has been Christianized while he is not and they come into conflict about certain things, like for example, the killing of the python. Now were there any specific instances, that you might have known from the point of view of history in your part of the country where these things happened – where a family was split by the teachings of two different cultures?

ACHEBE Oh yes there were such stories, yes, certainly, because the first generations of Christians (this is what I heard), had to demonstrate their faith in a very aggressive manner, and this often took the form of violating the customs of the village. At that stage there were skirmishes. But this was before my time. I heard of them, but on the whole I think the village accepted the new faith with humour. You see my great-grandfather for instance, was the man who had initially received the missionaries in my village. And he let them stay around and sing their songs; and eventually he said they must leave, not because of any conflict in religion, but because their singing sounded so mournful that his neighbours might think he was dead! And so they moved. But this was the kind of – I mean – good humour. After all, he even let my father join them.

SERUMAGA In your books you present the society as it is. Now in Africa there has been change to a certain extent, from the values of *Things Fall Apart* to the values of *A Man of the People*. Has this change been in the direction that you would have envisaged should be the right one?

ACHEBE Oh no, no, no, certainly not. Although you see life is not simple – it's often so complex. There have been gains – I mean let's not forget that, there have been gains, I am not one of those who would say that Africa has gained nothing at all during the colonial period, I mean this is ridiculous – we gained a lot. But unfortunately when two cultures meet, you would expect, if we were angels shall we say, we could pick out the best in the other and retain the best in our own, and this would be wonderful. But this doesn't happen often. What happens is that some of the worst elements of the old are retained and some of the worst of the new are added on to them. So if it were for me to order society I would be very unhappy about the way things have turned out. But again, I see this as the way life is. Every society has to grow up, every society has to learn its own lesson, so I don't despair. *A Man of the People* is a rather serious indictment – if you like – of post-independence Africa. But I don't give up because I think this is a necessary stage in our growth.

SERUMAGA You have hope. But do you see any agents of change; do you see bows behind the arrows of the gods, at the moment, to turn us into the right direction?

ACHEBE Oh yes, of course. I mean the coups, themselves, are bows shooting the arrows of God. If you take the example of Nigeria, which is the place I know best, things had got to such a point politically that there was no other answer – no way you could resolve this impasse politically. The political machine had been so abused that whichever way you pressed it, it produced the same results; and therefore you wanted another force, another force just had to come in. Now when I was writing *A Man of the People* it wasn't clear to me that this was going to be necessarily a military intervention. It could easily have been civil war, which in fact it very nearly was in Nigeria. But I think that all these things the next generation of politicians in Nigeria, when we do have them, will have experienced, and they'll have learned one or two lessons, I hope, from what happened to the First Republic. This is the only hope I have and if this turns out to be vain, it would really be terrible . . .

SERUMAGA Of course, you did almost uncannily predict the course of Nigerian events in *A Man of the People*, and in the earlier book, *Things Fall Apart*, it seemed to me that it was not the society itself that fell apart – the society was progressing or changing, if you like, in a dynamic sort of way culturally – and what fell apart, it seemed, was Okonkwo in his obstinacy; in his refusal to change at all it is Okonkwo who did completely break down. Would you agree with that?

ACHEBE Yes, I think this is a reasonable interpretation. I mean my sympathies were not entirely with Okonkwo – this is what I think you're getting at. Life just has to go on and if you refuse to accept changes, then tragic though it may be, you are swept aside.

SERUMAGA Of course the changes that came to the society in *Things Fall Apart* would have produced a situation where characters are no longer at ease, as in your next book. Now I must emphasize this because I'm terribly optimistic myself, I think that if we are going to change again, veer into another right direction, it's going to take us a long time. You don't agree with this at all?

ACHEBE I would neither agree nor disagree because I don't know how long it's going to take. I am not really concerned so much with whether it takes ten years or twenty years but with the final thing, and I am not being so naïve as to think that the progress is in one direction. You see, there are halts, there are even backward steps and so on, but I think in the final analysis writing is learning. Even if, mark you, this means a society breaks up, it may well be that this society had no basis for being together in the first place and this in itself is a lesson. We are learning for instance on the African scene that it's not enough to talk about unity and so on; you've got to work for it, you see, and 1966 was a disappointing year on the African scene. This I think is a necessary lesson.

SERUMAGA Now, going on to the other point about your writing: my assessment is that whereas earlier we had books that were almost apologetics of African culture, and then we had negritude which was a complete protest against Europe and the romanticization, almost, of African values, now you come with a kind of very confident approach whereby you present your society as it is, and therefore show us what is good in it and what is bad in it.

ACHEBE   I don't, in fact, remember consciously saying to myself that I must be confident. I saw that the kind of people I was writing about did not suffer any of these complexes – that brought about their excessive protestation or excessive whatever went on before. I found a number of people that were all around me who just lived their lives the way they wanted to live them, and these were the people I wanted to write about. It may be that at the back of my mind was this kind of decision that now we have had grovelling, we have had protest, now we must have something in between – I don't know, but I don't remember taking the decision consciously. That was the way I saw the story I was going to write, so that's how I wrote it.

SERUMAGA   Would it be that because the people in the society – and in a sense you yourself, say, writing about them – were in conditions where they hadn't been affected by the cultural changes which produced the writers of negritude, would it be that after your society of *Things Fall Apart* has been affected by these changes, that then these people themselves would have made the logical progression into a kind of negritude, a kind of protest against Europe, for the impositions Europe had made against them?

ACHEBE   Yes, I think in retrospect, I think I would agree. The working of the colonial period on Nigeria was rather different from its effect on, shall we say, Senegal. I think there is a certain difference in the way that Europe worked on Africa in various areas, and this is bound to create different responses.

SERUMAGA   Now, you mentioned earlier about how you work, you did not have this definite conception that you were going away from protest. How do you work when you are writing a novel like *Things Fall Apart* for instance; did you do a lot of research in the history of the society, or is it something you picked up from experience?

ACHEBE   This is largely picked up. As I said at the beginning this was the life that interested me, partly the life I lived and the life that was lived around me, supported by what I heard in conversation – I was very keen on listening to old people – and what I learned from my father, so it was all sort of picked up here and there. There was no research in the library if that's what you mean.

SERUMAGA   And how do you work with the language because you seem to get in all the authenticity of your particular language – in the way they speak, and transliterate it so beautifully into English. Now can you describe exactly how you do this, if you can?

ACHEBE   No, it's not easy. I feel consciously that if you were going to write about a certain character and I put down the dialogue between A and B, that somehow it would sound right or wrong and there's no way I can describe it except that it sounds wrong to my ear. If A talks like this and this is not right, I immediately feel it, that this is not right. I don't really see how else I can. . . .

SERUMAGA   There is no conscious intellectual process in transposing one language into another on your part?

ACHEBE   No, no, no. I just feel that this is the right way to convey this atmosphere, this speech or this idiom, this kind of language, you see. If you put in modern slang for instance, it would jar immediately.

SERUMAGA   It is said that you wrote *Things Fall Apart* in one go, with no revisions; is that true?

ACHEBE   Not altogether. My original conception of the story was really a combination of *Things Fall Apart* and *No Longer at Ease*. It was one story originally, not even long, it was short but it covered the whole period of *Things Fall Apart* and *No Longer at Ease*. And having done it I immediately felt that it was not right – that the time covered was too long and therefore the story was going to be too thin. So what I did was simply mechanically to cut it in two and blow up the first part. So there was that amount of rewriting, but not in detail. You see I work very slowly and carefully with my writing, so I don't have to do a first draft, a second draft and a third draft.

SERUMAGA   How long on average does it take you to finish a novel?

ACHEBE   Oh, it's varied from a year, even fourteen months, to five months.

SERUMAGA   And this is very interesting about your *Things Fall Apart* and *No Longer at Ease*, because I, as a reader, having read *Things Fall Apart* and *Arrow of God* and seen the references in *Things Fall Apart* to the python and the killing of the python and then seen this as the main theme of *Arrow of God*, I thought that *Arrow of God* was almost a continuation of the story of *Things Fall Apart* in a different context – with a different village. Would you say that this is so?

ACHEBE   Well, no, I don't think so. It is the same area – the supporting scenery is the same – it's got to be the same because I'm writing about the same people. So the supporting thing, the background is the same. But the story itself is not – in fact I see it as the exact opposite: Ezeulu the chief character in *Arrow of God* is a different kind of man from Okonkwo. He is an intellectual. He thinks about why things happen – of course as a priest; you see, his office requires this – so he goes into things, to the roots of things, and he's ready to accept change, intellectually. He sees the value of change and therefore his reaction to Europe is different, completely different, from

Okonkwo's. He is ready to come to terms with the new – up to a point – except where his dignity is involved. This he could not accept; he is very proud. So you see it's really the other side of the coin, and the tragedy is that they come to the same end, the same sort of sticky end. So there's really no escape whether you accept change or whether you don't – which is rather pessimistic, which I think should please you, although it is in fact not the same story.

SERUMAGA Well, does this then conflict with your own personal view of society?

ACHEBE It does only if you see it sort of fixed at one point. But if you take a long view of society, you will see that I think that it doesn't contradict what I said earlier, namely that if you take a long enough view, that society is, in fact, adjusting. Because life must go on, no matter what we say, no matter how many people suffer or how many people are killed, life does go on. This is really what I was saying at the beginning. But if you take a short episode, it may be full of tragedy. I mean if you take the situation in Nigeria today, it's full of tragedy – in Uganda even. But I think the long view, at least to me, holds out some element of hope.

SERUMAGA Well now, Chinua, you are no longer working with the radio of Nigeria. This presumably releases more of your time for writing, but why did you resign, and what are you going to do now?

ACHEBE I left radio in August last year as a result of the political situation – when it became unsafe to live in Lagos and I was terribly distressed with the turn of events, so I decided that the best thing was to leave. This decision was, of course, merely hastened by the political situation because I was already thinking that I had perhaps done enough in radio and I should be thinking of setting up as a full-time writer. And this is what I would like to do ultimately, although maybe for the next year or so I will probably work at the University of Nigeria at Nsukka, to help in setting up the Institute of African Literature which they're thinking about.

Ama Ata Aidoo
BORN 1942

▼▼▼▼▼▼▼▼▼▼▼▼▼▼▼▼▼▼▼▼▼▼▼▼▼▼▼▼

Interviewed by Maxine McGregor (née Lautré) in October 1967. This interview was recorded after Ama Ata Aidoo had been in the United States at the Harvard International Seminar. Her published work at the time of the interview consisted of the play *The Dilemma of a Ghost* (1965); her second play *Anowa* was complete and about to be published. She later published a collection of short stories, *No Sweetness Here*, in 1970.

LAUTRE   What do you think of the situation in America in arts?

AIDOO   The situation of America: in a way – it is very difficult for a foreigner to sum up the atmosphere. I think as a black person I could see two definite, clear, almost unallied paths, and this new insight I gained, not only from the seminar, but from the opportunity I had later on to travel through the country, to get to know more of it. One of them is what I would call the white *avant-garde* – all the hippies, the 'new thing', which is very vibrant, carefree, almost, 'irresponsible'. It is interesting to watch, because, in a way, thinking about this hippie movement and everything, of all the writers in the world, I think of Françoise Sagan because to me the same kind of envy I entertain for Sagan as a writer is the same type of envy I entertain for the hippie movement because it is the type of nice thing you would do if you had the chance.

LAUTRE   You mean it's not really practical.

AIDOO   It comes with freedom – a certain type of freedom which I think no black person in this world has right now. It's almost like doing something which is beautiful and nice because you want to do it – like writing a story about lovers in Paris – it is beautiful, it is nice. But whereas Sagan could do it, and she does do it with a whole lot of relevance and validity, I cannot see myself as a writer, writing about lovers in Accra because you see, there are so many other problems . . .

LAUTRE   You feel a responsibility in fact.

AIDOO   Exactly. You know, I feel a responsibility and I feel that it's the same type of responsibility I think black people all over feel. I mean who cares about lovers in Accra, whereas we do care about lovers in Paris because it's another side of human nature and existence which we can enjoy if people are not caught up in other problems.

LAUTRE   That's quite interesting, and the other side now – you think that was the one side?

AIDOO   Ah! yes, the other side, well, is the whole black movement.

LAUTRE   The Black Power thing?

AIDOO   Yes. Well, yes, the Black Power thing, but since that is political, I'd choose here not to use the word 'Black *Power*', but to refer to the black phenomenon in its more artistic form; I'd say that there is this black awareness in art, in everything, you know.

LAUTRE   Do you feel that it's sort of strong at the moment?

AIDOO   Yes, I think that there's almost a desire, a need, an awareness on the part of black Americans to have their own standards in art, in literature because most of them say that they are just tired of being described by white America as – 'The only negro writer, blah-blah-blah-blah blah', 'The best negro writer . . .', you know, everything . . .

LAUTRE   . . . to be valued on their own terms?

AIDOO   Exactly. This need. This fight to be valid on their own terms, despite what anybody would say. It's almost that they want to say, 'Now this is what we say we like, we value; you take it or leave it.' – It's a growing thing.

LAUTRE   Did you meet some of the writers? Who for instance?

AIDOO   Well, I met Leroy Jones fleetingly, and I didn't really have any discussion with him. I met a fantastic poet coming out of San Francisco – Anthony Towers . . . He was jailed for long time, then he came out. When he came out, he came out with a volume of poetry – the most fantastic stuff I've ever seen. And then I found one of my friends in Stanford – happened to be John Scott, one of those, in quotes, 'Watts poets', you know.

LAUTRE   Did you come across any of the Ghanaians or Nigerians in America, I mean, are they doing anything very much or . . . ?

AIDOO   Not really. You know, the few Ghanaians I met are normal students about their business, that kind of thing. I didn't meet with any Ghanaian writers there.

LAUTRE   But you've seen Joe Okpaku, who has that magazine.* What do you think of that?

AIDOO   Oh, I think that his magazine is good to have around. I can't say any more than that. If I had the money to set up a magazine, it might be different, but then it's because we see a few things in different ways. Still, I think it's a good magazine – I mean it's a solid thing, and I hope he will be able to carry on with it – have it even more firmly established than it is

* *The Journal of the New African Literature and Arts* (JONALA) – Stanford. It has now ceased publication. Okpaku is Nigerian.

already. I think Joe is a fantastic sort of worker and I find it almost incredible that within a short time he decided to have a magazine and there you have it! It's the kind of ability I don't think I've got.

LAUTRE   And he's very young too.

AIDOO   Very young. And he is a prolific writer. Joe is really good to have, you know – without meaning to sound patronizing, because I'm not even much older than him. I mean, he is a refreshing somebody to really have around. It's good to meet someone like Joe who gets things done. If you gave me the opportunity, it would take me five years to bring out my issue. It's true and it's not a boast!

LAUTRE   Now, before you went to America, what were you doing at the Institute of African Studies at the University of Ghana?

AIDOO   I was teaching – I was sort of offered a fellowship to enable me to write and then I was doing a bit of research on contemporary Ghanaian drama ... a kind of drama in Fanti, which has been going on long, since the thirties, you know. ... It caters for at least a clear 80 per cent of the people in the country because most Ghanaians including even those in the North can understand some form of Akan and they can certainly enjoy the action because there's a lot of it. 'The Trio' – this is the name of the drama, you know – is for the people. In fact, it is the people's drama.

LAUTRE   Is it folk drama?

AIDOO   It is folk drama. The nearest thing I've heard that is akin to it in a Western sense is vaudeville. I don't know much about vaudeville so I could not fully endorse my own analogy unless I knew more about vaudeville. But it uses music, singing, dancing ...

LAUTRE   Is it anything like the folk opera in Nigeria?

AIDOO   It's the same I think, except that in Ghana it's called 'The Trio'. They originally used only three actors each of whom fell into the various parts. Sometimes it has a rough script but much of it is improvised. Practically, it only uses male actors even for female parts. Much of it is exaggerated drama; like, a man might be with a woman. The woman says, 'Husband, I have been waiting for you'; in 'Trios' the man would say (in a feminine voice), 'Oh my dear husband, I've been waiting for you for such a very long time,' you know, because everything is exaggerated; it's that kind of drama. And they use lots of make-up.

LAUTRE   Are there some companies like Duro Ladipo or Ogunmola?*

AIDOO   Exactly. In Ghana Bob Cole is well known, and Kakiku, and Nyame. You know, I think it is the most valid thing going. I feel almost guilty myself writing the type of thing I write really. ...

LAUTRE   On the other hand one wants to do a lot of things, and there

* Nigerian folk-opera Director-actor-manager.

aren't an awful lot of writers in Ghana at the moment writing in English, I think, are there?

AIDOO   No, and my own sort of alibi for wanting to continue writing in English is, well, one gets the chance for communicating with other Africans outside of Ghana, even in Ghana alone, say you are writing in English, you are more able to carry yourself over – if you have any message – carry your message over to more people outside.

LAUTRE   Efua Sutherland, is she working with them or not? What exactly is she doing?

AIDOO   Much of her own writing has been in English. But, in fact she has been doing research into Ghanaian – Ghana drama built upon traditional forms like the Anansi folktale. What she conceives, and I agree with her to a great extent, is that you take the narration – the traditional narration of a folktale. In the course of the narration, you get a whole lot of dramatic behaviour which one should use, in writing plays even in English. I mean, it's complicated to explain but I believe with her that in order for African drama to be valid, it has to derive lots of its impetus, its strength, from traditional African dramatic forms, however one conceives these forms, because they exist. What we must do is to find out what they are, and how we can use them and she's been working in this type of field.

LAUTRE   Has she written any plays recently?

AIDOO   No, but she is publishing one of her old plays very soon.

LAUTRE   Do you think that she will, when she's done a bit more research, come out with something?

AIDOO   I hope she will because if there's anyone in Ghana who knows anything about what should happen, I think it's her.

LAUTRE   What about now, someone like Mauriseau Le Roi; what is that theatrical tradition doing?

AIDOO   Right now I haven't the slightest idea what he is doing now, but as you know, he is a Haitian and he too has a great deal of belief in African traditional drama. And what he was doing was trying to incorporate some of those forms as he saw them.

LAUTRE   Successful?

AIDOO   Well, you know, to a certain extent. As far as it is possible for a non-Ghanaian to be able to do a thing like that – he was successful, but right now I don't know ...

LAUTRE   Are there any others – is there any theatre in Accra besides the Trios – not really?

AIDOO   Yes there is a modern one – the general African theatre in English. There was – the theatre built in Ghana, The Drama Studio, which was producing plays written by, you know, Africans or non-Africans in English.

The director of the theatre is Joe de Graft* and right now he is also the kind of head of the Drama Department in the Institute of African Studies. This theatre is like any of the African theatres in English producing plays by Africans now and then. A play by anybody who is interesting. They produced Brecht's 'Mother Courage' and they've produced 'Madame Butterfly' . . .

LAUTRE Have they produced your play?

AIDOO I heard 'The Dilemma' had two productions in the University – not by the Drama Studio.

LAUTRE Where else has it been produced?

AIDOO Well, it was produced in Nigeria, in Lagos, I understand, Ibadan and Nsukka last year, and I also know that it had been produced in a couple of schools in Ghana.

LAUTRE What is the new play called?

AIDOO 'Anowa.'

LAUTRE 'Anowa' and what's that about? Is it on a similar theme to "Dilemma" or quite different?

AIDOO No, this is very different from 'The Dilemma'. This is set in the latter part of the nineteenth century in what was then the Gold Coast, and it's more or less my own rendering of a kind of . . . legend, because, according to my mother, who told me the story, it is supposed to have happened. The ending is my own and the interpretation I give to the events that happen is mine . . . A girl married a man her people did not approve of; she helped him become fantastically rich, and then he turns round to sort of drive her away. The original story I heard, which in a way was in the form of a song, didn't say why he did this, and I myself provide an answer to this, a clue, you know, a kind of pseudo-Freudian answer. . . .

LAUTRE I wanted to ask you about the poetry. I was thinking of that article you wrote in *The New African*.

AIDOO What did I say in the article – I think I discussed, you know, the existence of African poetic forms for one thing, and the need for a kind of redefinition of poetry – the whole idea that poetry has to conform to certain accepted Western standards. One doesn't have to really assume that all literature has to be written. I mean one doesn't have to be so patronizing about oral literature. There is a present validity to oral literary communication. I totally disagree with people who feel that oral literature is one stage in the development of man's artistic genius. To me it's an end in itself. One can recite to people; even today with all the facilities for writing and stuff like that, I mean if I had my way really what I would be interested in is a form of theatre where you don't only have to produce a play – where

* Joe de Graft has since gone to Kenya to work on a UNESCO theatre project.

you can just sit down and relate a story. They don't have to be folktales only, there are lots of stories going around. In fact I believe that when a writer writes a short story, it should be possible for the writer to sit before an audience and tell them the story of a boy and a girl in Accra, or London, or Paris. I believe this so strongly; if I have any strong conception of what else could be done in literature, it is this. We don't always have to write for readers, we can write for listeners.

LAUTRE Do you see any possibility of being able to do theatre like this in Ghana?

AIDOO Lots and lots and lots of possibilities. I think if you announce today – even if you put on a series of short stories or a series of poems, you will get an audience.

LAUTRE Do you think you might do this?

AIDOO If I had the money or the position – what I mean is I don't have any facility. If I had the facilities, this is what I would want to do; set up a theatre – preferably in Accra because this is the kind of context I know best – and just go right on ahead. I feel so strongly – it's my thing. If I don't have a play around, I will invite people to come to listen to poetry, either in English or in Fanti, or to come to listen to tales, folktales, or modern stories – entertain them – I mean this is my concept of entertainment. In fact I pride myself on the fact that my stories are written to be heard, primarily.

LAUTRE You'd like to be able to communicate verbally and have the written thing if people can't be there.

AIDOO Exactly. What I mean is that if I have a good short story by somebody, I would want to either have the person reading it to an audience or telling it to an audience. We cannot tell our stories maybe with the same expertise as our forefathers. But to me, all the art of the speaking voice could be brought back so easily. We are not that far away from our traditions. Now I could either have the person himself telling or reading it to an audience or get a good reader to read it to an audience. If anyone is interested in what I would want to do really with my life as an artist, this is what I would want to do. Give me a theatre . . . On a very small scale, I even thought of – of all things, setting up an African sort of kitchen with a restaurant for African food, and a kind of backyard – a kind of big patio, where people in the evening would come and sit and tell stories, do plays, read poetry . . .

LAUTRE You need something a bit like the Mbari, Oshogbo?

AIDOO Exactly, in fact . . .

LAUTRE A communal centre.

AIDOO Exactly.

LAUTRE Well you never know, it could come true. What do you think of the future of African literature in other parts of Africa apart from Ghana, I mean the writers and so on? Or is that very difficult?

AIDOO Oh no. The thing is that I think the world is going to be literarily deluged with African material. In fact, now that Africans have got the idea that they can express themselves, whether in writing in their own languages or in a second language, they're just going to go on, I mean go on and on and on until someone says, 'For heaven's sake!' True, I feel people are going to write and write and just write.

Now there are going to be problems; one is, you know, whether the few interested publishing houses are going to be able to absorb all the material, since national publishing houses are not that many in Africa; what I mean is that when you are writing for a foreign publishing house, you have a big problem you know. You may write something which they do not fancy or they may just say, 'We can't do it any more.' I think this is going to be one big problem.

The other big problem is the whole business of what this literature is going to be. We are all sick – I am – with all the expert theories about the nature of modern African poetry, you know, modern African literature. That will have to stop, but no one can stop that sort of thing apart from the writers themselves. I do not see that there is any validity in having someone who does not belong to the society from which the literature itself springs, telling you how to write. I'm sure you've heard every African writer say this, but I do not see how it can work. What I mean is; if the writing is from a certain background, it's only the people who are from the background who can tell the world, 'this is good', and then the world takes it. To me it's so simple one doesn't even have to talk about it. You know, nobody else but the English critical world could say that John Osborne is a good playwright. Now when you get England recognizing Osborne as good or bad, at any rate controversial, then other people become interested. You see what I mean?

LAUTRE How are you going to solve this problem? I mean, do you think that there should be more national publishing houses, or that the other, foreign publishing houses should have African officials so that they could themselves . . .

AIDOO I think that: one – we should have more publishing houses; but then who is Ama Ata Aidoo: I'm not a policy maker for anybody. So, if you ask me, yes I think we should have more publishing houses; two – the publishing houses should try to have African readers. But all this is really sort of pre-dating the most important problem, and that is, we should have the African intellectuals or whatever you call the crowd, the readership, made more interested in African writers because it is only when you get them reading that you are also going to get them to say whether they like this or they don't.

LAUTRE   How are you going to make them more interested?

AIDOO   Put them in the school books.

LAUTRE   Isn't there a sort of syllabus of African literature?

AIDOO   Yes, in a few universities, but you see, as yet Africans have not even understood that African writers are to be read. You see what I mean? We are still so primitive and I'm using this word – what I mean is – not to say the Western notion of African primitiveness, with our grass skirts but I mean, you know, we are so . . . uncomfortable. . . . You come to literature or things like that, and it's then that you really understand a term like neo-colonialism. We are so, so gauche? Because of the colonial experience we still, unfortunately, are very much lacking in confidence in ourselves and what belongs to us. It's beautiful to have independence, but it's what has happened to our minds that is to me the most frightening thing about the colonial experience. Until quite recently, we thought that a book was written by a white man . . .

LAUTRE   Anything African is not much good or —

AIDOO   Yes, or that they are not even capable of doing anything and this is the reason why I love Achebe: that, you know, he gave so much – to me anyway he gave so much in confidence – it doesn't matter what you think about his writing. You know, what I mean is that when I read *Things Fall Apart* I said, 'Oh, so! He can do this' and I went to my English lecturer and said, 'Are we going to study it for our degree?' You see! This was my initial reaction.

LAUTRE   I think Eldred Jones has got a very good idea of doing that in Sierra Leone. I think that's probably what is needed – a lot of people like that in the Universities really.

AIDOO   Exactly because these are the spear heads of the literary movement. If you get your university undergraduates interested in these things, then they will carry them over to the schools where they are going to teach. In Ghana the whole idea of school drama is very firmly fixed. You know in most schools at least you have one play produced every year. Now if you get your university students interested, when they go to teach as English teachers or something, when the question of drama comes, at least the possibility also exists in their minds that one can do *Hamlet* but then one can also do Soyinka and they also make their pupils aware of these things right from the beginning and then it goes on. But if your English Departments are staffed with people, black or white, who do not know too much about these things and couldn't care anyway, then you have this same lack of knowledge, lack of interest, enthusiasm, self-confidence, you know, perpetuated.

LAUTRE Another tack now, Ama. You are studying French intensively now, are you interested in the French African writers?

AIDOO Yes, very much. I think really it's almost – well this is another of my pet subjects. I think it's almost suicidal – self-defeating or whatever, for anyone messing around with things African unless they are bilingual, at least with French and English. I find myself terribly handicapped, you know, so I think at least that I should make an effort to learn French.

LAUTRE My great grandfather was French, also my father speaks very good French but I've never learnt properly. If I go to France I can understand what they are talking about. But again I find to read a French book is such a battle.

AIDOO Oh! then you don't even enjoy it. Yes, this is what I intend to do, you know.

Kofi Awoonor
GEORGE AWOONOR WILLIAMS
BORN 1935

▼▼▼▼▼▼▼▼▼▼▼▼▼▼▼▼▼▼▼▼▼▼▼▼▼▼▼▼▼

At the time of this interview with Robert Serumaga in London in March 1967, Kofi Awoonor was Director of the Ghana Film Corporation. He has published essays and poems in various magazines and anthologies. His main works consist of *Rediscovery*, published by Mbari in 1964 – a collection of poems. He has since co-edited with George Adali-Mortty an anthology of Ghanaian poetry, *Messages, Poems from Ghana*, published by Heinemann, London, 1971. A novel *This Earth, My Brother* (Heinemann, London, 1972) has been published, as well as a second volume of poetry, *Night of My Blood*. Kofi Awoonor started writing under the name George Awoonor Williams.

AWOONOR *We have found a new land*
  The smart professionals in three piece
  Sweating away their humanity in driblets
  And wiping the blood from their brow
  We have found a new land
  This side of eternity
  Where our blackness does not matter
  And our songs are dying on our lips.
  Standing at hellgate you watch those who seek admission
  Still the familiar faces that watched and gave you up
  As the one who had let the side down
  'Come on, old boy, you cannot dress like that'
  And tears well in my eyes for them
  These who want to be seen in the best company
  Have adjured the magic of being themselves
  And in the new land we have found
  The water is drying from the towel.
  Our songs are dead and we sell them dead to the other side
  Reaching for the Stars we stop at the house of Moon
  And pause to relearn the wisdom of our fathers.

SERUMAGA   This is one of your poems. Does it sum up your opinions about the Africa before, the present Africa, and the Africa to come?

AWOONOR   Yes it does, to a very large extent. You can see I was talking and what I was saying in this poem is really that the problem of adjustment for the new African, if there is anything like that, the new African who is caught up in the world of Europe, in the world of the white man, with a ballot-box, with a new outfit, clothes, and with a parliament, with a national anthem, and a song, what is he going to do about the wisdom of his fathers? And this is what I was trying to mirror in this particular part.

SERUMAGA   And what do you think he is going to do about the wisdom of his fathers in the new circumstances?

AWOONOR   This is a very difficult question. I have a strong feeling that on whatever level you are going to discuss a subject like this, the political, or the social, or the economic level, one invariably returns to a certain basic aspect, which is the technological advancement of Africa, and all the things that are added on to it: what are we going to do with some of the basic traditions of African life, African communal life, the general spirit that did motivate African societies long before the white man came? And I see in this a simple answer which is not going to be described in political terms, that one has to adjust one's self to the thinking, the way of life which has almost died, to marry it to this new technology; I am thinking particularly about the traditions and customs and observances, and also positively about relationships to one another.

SERUMAGA   How much are you yourself, first as a person in your society, and secondly as a writer, influenced by the old traditions of the society in which you live?

AWOONOR   Tremendously. I have always felt, perhaps involuntarily, I should take my poetic sensibility if you like the word, from the tradition that sort of feeds my language, because in my language there is a lot of poetry, there is a lot of music and there is a lot of the literary art, even though not written, and so I take my cue from this old tradition, and begin to break it into English, to give it a new dimension as it were.

SERUMAGA   Can you describe exactly how you get from your language on to English? Is this a deliberate intellectual exercise or is it an inspiration which fires into you certain different images and phrases that you are not consciously trying to translate?

AWOONOR   Really, when I started writing, a few years back, I remember very well, that I started with some old songs, which I had learned or heard from my grandmother and this had been the basis. I translated these and tried to put them in English, but then of course, the incentive comes from that level, from that point, almost like a point of impact, and you begin to create in English, with this in mind. This, as it were, informs it.

SERUMAGA   You say in one of your poems, 'The Anvil and the Hammer', you say 'Caught between the anvil and the hammer | In the forging house of a new life | Transforming the pangs that delivered me | Into the joy of new songs.' Are you very conscious that you are, in fact, in a difficult position – trying to marry two cultures – or do you just tend to let them shape you, rather than your trying to bring things together in a deliberate sort of way?

AWOONOR   I think both; I'm trying primarily to let me fashion, as I said in this poem, to, as it were, break out, to build a new thing which already is there perhaps without my being aware of it. And then I'm letting this new thing become the view or the attitude that is going to push me into this world within which I find myself, willy-nilly.

SERUMAGA   Well now, how difficult do you find this? I mean, does it impose on you a sort of neurosis about what is this whole thing about. Am I going to achieve it? Or does it come easily to you?

AWOONOR   It does impose its own type of neurosis; after all, I have been brought up in English literature, and this is a stumbling block to the exercise of forging a new medium, forging a new language, because I regard it as a new language, because one is thinking about one's own language at the same time as one is thinking about English, and how are you going to express your views, express your sentiments, perhaps not bothering so much about the larger aspects of the question, but as an individual in this situation. Of course, it has its little neuroses here and there, and the question of adjusting yourself to it.

SERUMAGA   Now, apart from the individual trying to adjust himself to this situation, how do you see the African society itself, trying to transform itself under the new circumstances? Is it succeeding, or is it, in your view, failing to do this?

AWOONOR   Well, I think it was one of the African leaders who talked about us having to sort of jet-propel ourselves into the twentieth century, and this is a fact; and within this process of jet-propelling ourselves into the twentieth century, we are going to commit all kinds of blunders, and the blunders are self-evident in the situation which Africa is in today. Politically or socially, the whole question of economic organizations and social organizations, or political institutions, has really come out to show that we have not had our education properly in terms of what we are trying to do; we become black Europeans, either black Frenchmen as you see in most of the French-speaking African countries, or black Englishmen as you see in most of the English-speaking African countries. But I think there is a medium somewhere, there is a centre somewhere, where some kind of security is going to be achieved which has no relationship with political institutions – either political ideologies or concepts of democracy, or what not and so on. Those concepts might come in handy and useful, but then the basis is going invariably to be found in the society which we are trying to change, the society which is going to drive jet air-planes, and is going to use railways and is going to build harbours and so on.

SERUMAGA In this social philosophy, and political philosophy of the Africans, they do many times use the old traditions to justify, to sort of link up with the new traditions. I was thinking of Nkrumah's *Consciencism*, for example, and Willy Abraham's book about the African mind. Now, do you sometimes find, in fact, that a lot of the politicians, having committed a mistake of policy, tend to go back and justify it by some almost irrelevant link in tradition; say, for example, you might find socialism declared in certain parts of the country and on the continent without any real conviction of the socialism as we know it, but it is justified in terms of the communalism of the old society. Do you think this is true?

AWOONOR Yes, I think I would describe this as sheer chicanery in a way, because if we are talking about socialism, or scientific socialism, or Marxist-Leninism, you are talking about something which is already there and positively spelt out. You've got to talk about something else, other than these other 'isms! Nkrumah tried to bring out something he called 'Nkrumahism' which was a hotch-potch of all kinds of things. On the other hand, people qualify a European ideology with the adjective 'African', and this time my mind sort of slinks back to Nyerere, who talks about African socialism – he uses a Swahili word for it, 'Ujamaa', which to me doesn't make sense, because if you're going to forge out a political theory, in relationship to a society which is, as it were, waking up into the twentieth century, I would believe that you are going to take up the search for the positives of that society, and at the same time begin also to feel that you have to make it a twentieth-century society, and the positives are not necessarily the business of societies or peoples sitting together and having communal meals and so on, and hoeing each other's farm together and that sort of thing, because these are not going to be compatible with this new society which is a twentieth-century society in which you're trying to propel it.

SERUMAGA Yes. Now here is the African situation as you have just described it with the political philosophy being replaced by a kind of militarism, and on the other side you have the writing within which certain people are trying to forge a new kind of African writing in English or in French. Do you think they are succeeding very much? Can you point to particular examples which in your view have succeeded in doing this?

AWOONOR   You mean African writing?

SERUMAGA   African writing.

AWOONOR   Well, I would say yes; there are a lot of African writers who have really succeeded. I think readily of somebody like Wole Soyinka. I read Wole Soyinka and have a feeling that he's not exactly writing English – he's got a hybrid of Yoruba strength which is married to English which he uses very well; and I think about Chinua Achebe, and I think of J. P. Clark; I will not mention others, but I feel that African writing is moving; it's moving about say four or five generations into a new field which is going to mean that African writers are going to go back and find materials and inspiration in their own societies to write about. They move from the period of Osadebay* and Michael Dei-Anang† and so on, the political writing, to personal writing which is going to be defined as writing committed to a certain positive aspect of African life.

SERUMAGA   Do you think that in this going back to the roots – the way you have just described it: finding inspiration within this particular society, that it probably would bring with it, at the same time, going back to writing in the local languages rather than in English and French?

AWOONOR   Yes, I will say that there is going to break out – there has always been – a lot of writing in the vernaculars, but I would not put too much faith in this because it sort of peters out into small linguistic groups which are going to read and understand this specific type of writing; but English or French or Portuguese have been transplanted into African societies.

SERUMAGA   The problem that emerges here is that the more African, as it were, one gets – the writer gets – in English or French or Portuguese, the more difficult does it become for the person who is not from that particular area of Africa to understand. I'm now thinking of things like *Arrow of God*, in which a person like myself from Uganda, although an African, finds it quite difficult to understand certain bits of the reasoning and proverbs and things like that. Now what I'm thinking is, if we go right back to be inspired by this language, won't we then be creating a kind of

* Dennis Chukude Osadebay (b. 1911, Nigeria), published a volume *Africa Sings* in the 1930s, four poems from which are represented in Donatus Nwoga's *West African Verse* (Longmans, 1967).

† Michael F. Dei-Anang (b. 1909, Ghana), writings include two published plays and four volumes of verse: *Wayward Lines from Africa* (1946), *Africa Speaks*, *Ghana Semi-tones* (Presbyterian Bk. Depot, 1962) and *Ghana Glory* – (with Yaw Warren) (Nelson, London, 1965).

English that is really not English but is an African kind of English. This would be narrowing our audience, wouldn't you think?

AWOONOR   Yes, it would be narrowing our audience, but at the same time I have a feeling that this has to be done very carefully. I think readily of Cyprian Ekwensi and his book, *Jagua Nana* which makes a lot of sense to a very large West African audience. This is as large as is possible for Cyprian to reach, but if he did write say in Yoruba or Ibo (I think Ibo is his native language) he is going to be circumscribed now, or limited to a much smaller society; so there is a positive side to this too, that if you write in a very localized English or French, you are going to reach out to a larger audience than if you do write in Ewe or in Fanti or in Yoruba or in Hausa or Ibo.

SERUMAGA   This is very true, and I do think that the writers you have mentioned probably do achieve this; but I think that J. P. Clark, for example, sometimes becomes so involved that to a person who doesn't come from that particular area where J. P. Clark comes from, his work becomes quite difficult. I'm thinking of lines from 'The Raft', you've got lines like, 'What mystery! Even the night masquerade | So full of the lion's roar and jackal's howl | Is but sharpened bamboo shafts swinging about | The heads of boys proclaiming their puberty.' Now, this is in a play which one plays to an audience which is not from Nigeria or even not from Africa, and one might as well speak the African language, as far as I can see in this particular instance, because the audience is completely excluded. How do you solve that kind of thing?

AWOONOR   Well, I do not think that there is a need at all to begin to try to solve this sort of thing because I think it should be allowed to go ahead. After all, when we read about 'daffodils' and 'the timid hares' in English poetry or any outlandish stuff as that in English poetry, or any other literature of Europe, our perceptions were so limited that we were able to catch only very little aspects of these things in terms of understanding and meaning; and I should think that this is a positive side of this type of writing of, say, J. P. Clark or of Wole Soyinka in his very difficult play, a play which people discover is very difficult, namely *A Dance of the Forests*, which I could understand very easily because in one aspect it's simply a kind of cycle of events cutting through the history of a people; and this makes a lot of meaning to me if you see some of the traditional performances of any society in West Africa.

SERUMAGA   Yes. I think I agree with you there entirely because one gets imposed upon by European critics, and one gets the kind of neurosis which tends to dictate to him that he must explain himself to be understood. . . .

AWOONOR   That's right.

SERUMAGA   ... which I think would be the death of what we are trying to do in African literature. Now, what about the poets in Africa? We haven't mentioned any specific names except, of course, J. P. Clark who is a poet, as well as Soyinka, but what about the others?

AWOONOR   Well, the poets – I think a lot of individual poetry is being written at the moment, individual poetry which at the same time takes up busy questions of commitment, busy questions as to why, how and to what you are committed in your society. I'm thinking of someone like Kwesi Brew* whose beautiful poem, 'Ancestral Faces', conjures to me, in fact sums up, some of my own ideas about our ancestors returning and recognizing us, seeing that we haven't changed at all; all that we've got perhaps is a few lines of railways and a few harbours, and we're dancing the same dances and singing the same songs; and to me this is very fresh. But I would not subscribe to the practice which sort of shifts itself into the extremity of individualism, like what you find in some of Chris Okigbo's poetry, for example, most of which is highly, I think, derivative, and at the same time quaint, because if you pick up T. S. Eliot or Ezra Pound or anybody you could think that these were written by these same people, except with very peculiar turns of phrases here and there. But I should think that a writer is going to be concerned with a certain aspect of his society or the whole society in relationship to himself, and basically because I feel his genius is going to be fed upon a tradition which has moved from the oral into the written.

SERUMAGA   Well, yes, it's good that you should mention Chris Okigbo because he on the other hand – I took him to task on this myself – and he says that he is in fact trying to be himself in a way that you've just described; and this is what comes out of him from his education, his involvement in his own society, and if, for instance, the classical influences, the modern European influences are expressed, it is natural, for what will also flow out is the influence of the Ibo society in which he lived – and that what he writes as a result is what comes out of him naturally. Now he says that if he tried to sort of get away from the European influences which would seem at the moment to be derivative he would not be 'being himself'.† Would you think that this was a fair explanation of what he writes?

---

* O. H. Kwesi Brew (b. 1928, Ghana) whose collection of poetry *The Shadows of Laughter* (Longmans, 1968), contains 'Ancestral Faces' as well as all the Kwesi Brew poems in Donatus Nwoga's *West African Verse*, Awoonor and Adali-Mortty's 'Messages', and most of those of his poems in *Poetry from Africa* (Pergamon Poets 2, Pergamon Press, 1968) ed. Howard Sergeant.

† Cf. interview with Okigbo, pp. 143–147.

AWOONOR   I think so; I think it's a very fair explanation, except that he doesn't conform with my own attitude, or my own answer to the perennial question of, 'Is the African writer going to be committed to anything in his society, or to what is he going to be committed? Is he going to be involved in the development and the progress, or retrogression of his society?' Basically if he is going to let himself be imposed upon by the Western influences, as against his traditional African influences, then I would say it's a pity because he might have had a peculiarly difficult type of education which will, as it were, tear him root and branch from his sources. There's an element of alienation.

SERUMAGA   But supposing an African writer came to you and said, 'Look, I have been educated strictly in the European way, you see, and this is what I am.' Would you condemn him, or would you say 'What a pity!' Or what would you do?

AWOONOR   I would say, 'What a pity!' I used to know a chap at home, an oldish chap, who has been writing since the thirties, who did write some poetry in Latin ... and some of these had been published. I don't hold it against him. Probably at that period in which he was writing he was very much strongly influenced by Roman Catholicism, or by any institutions that might have fashioned his writing in that direction. But I would feel that the need is there for a very ... perhaps not a deliberately conscious ... but a very conscious return to one's roots.

SERUMAGA   How do you yourself work? You seem to have a job in a film unit, and then you write and you travel quite a lot. How do you fit in these things into your life? How do you divide your time?

AWOONOR   In fact, my work at the moment doesn't allow me much time to write at all, and this, I find, is a great pity, and as soon as I can, if I can leave this job, and devote my time to writing, I shall; but then I must earn a living, because writing cannot afford a living for one in Africa.

SERUMAGA   Yes. This is the other very difficult problem. What do you think is going to be done about this question? It is, on the one hand, probably bad to subsidize writers, and on the other hand, a writer has got to have time to be able to write, and to devote more time to this means he makes less and less of a living. How do you think we're going to solve this?

AWOONOR   I really can't see the way out. I still see it simply that one of the factors that might be important is that African writers who are producing worthwhile works could get into some kind of a continental foundation which would allow them periods of say one year, or two years to write and then go back to a job which has something to do with writing, or the theatre, where they don't sort of dry up; because if you're a civil servant sitting behind a desk and you're supposed to be writing plays for the theatre, the divergence is so great that you're really going to have a very tough time trying to produce.

SERUMAGA What are you planning to do in the very near future? Are you going to leave a job and take up writing, or are you not going to leave a job?

AWOONOR This is a very difficult question; I can't answer it at the moment. I'm giving myself another four months or so within which I might make a decision.

When this interview was recorded with Dennis Duerden in October 1968, Kofi Awoonor was studying for a B.Litt. degree at University College, London. After this he became Professor of English at the State University of New York, Stony Brook. This interview is limited to a discussion of the oral origins of high life songs and of Awoonor's poetry.

It was during this period that, amongst other work, Awoonor wrote a series of short plays and sketches, two of which are to be published in *Short African Plays* edited by Cosmo Pieterse, Heinemann, London, 1972.

DUERDEN Can you begin by saying something about popular music in Ghana, the songs that we know as high life songs, and what sort of influence they've had in the modern political situation?

AWOONOR Yes, one will have to go back a few years, at least to the period when political agitation began in Ghana in the late forties and early fifties. When Nkrumah had his Convention People's Party, there was always a musician, a band, E. K. Nyame who's still very much on the scene, the musical scene in Ghana, who was, as it were the official musician of the Convention People's Party, and anywhere they had a rally, E.K. was on his platform with the boys, and they made up songs and so on – praise songs, songs of taunt to the opposition, and generally kept the spirit of what Nkrumah was saying moving in music.

DUERDEN Have these musicians played any part in the opposition to Nkrumah?

AWOONOR Yes, I remember very well when Busia was in exile, there was a famous song called 'Osu Beto Mframa Di Kay' which means 'When it's going to rain, the wind blows. I told you and you did not believe me.' And this song was played for Ghanaians. I think it was played on the BBC, as a kind of 'Listeners' Choice' programme, requested by Busia for

Ghanaians, and the immediate repercussion was that this song was banned by the Nkrumah government, that is, it was banned officially. It was not allowed to be played on the radio in Ghana.

DUERDEN I believe there were some cases, though, of songs which were sung on the radio and the Convention People's Party weren't aware that they had this meaning. I mean, that you have songs with double meanings.

AWOONOR Yes, yes. This is very true. This was the famous song called 'Mansa Wo Mba' which was a song which was saying, 'Mansa, your children are fighting' – and it sort of went on, picked it up in this traditional pattern, saying 'Mansa there you are, your children whom you've left behind, they're having to undergo so much suffering', and 'Where is the help, where is the succour coming from, to redeem them from this condition?' and of course nobody would seriously analyse this song, but the composers and the musicians knew exactly what they were saying.

DUERDEN But, well presumably eventually, the people that this song was directed at were going to find out what song was being sung and what it meant.

AWOONOR Yes, yes. When a few months ago there was a kind of political upheaval in Ghana, when a few rebel soldiers of the army wanted to take over the government after the first coup, the song that they used was a high life song. The operation was called Operation Guitar Boy and immediately 'Operation Guitar Boy' became a very popular song in Ghana, and I used to go to the Star Hotel, and the Star Hotel was jam-packed with people, and there were people shouting, requesting 'Operation Guitar Boy'. Of course, they didn't have any direct political meaning. Now, of course, I don't know what the situation is at the moment, but one sort of hears that people are composing a lot of high life which sort of is saying 'Well – we didn't really bargain for this kind of situation. Perhaps we've made a mistake!' Well, however well-formed that kind of sentiment is, it's yet to be discussed, or discovered.

DUERDEN Now, what I'm particularly interested in is the ways in which this kind of singing has arisen from traditions, from what has happened in the past. It seems to me impossible that singing should play such an important part in modern African politics and not have played an important role in the past, and in fact, if we have a look at the past, we can discover some important sources of this kind of singing. Now, I believe that in your own societies, in the Akan societies and the societies of your own people there are various commoners' associations referred to as the Asafo. This is the correct name in both societies, is it?

AWOONOR Yes. This is the correct name in both societies. Now, in the modern political situation in Ghana, in particular, one has always had a condition in which the musicians play a very important role in the political life of the country. They sort of generate a kind of spontaneous awareness of politics and a spontaneous awareness of the hazards of politics, the chicanery of politicians and whatnot and they put it in songs, they put it in music, they dramatize it. You have the concert parties who dramatize political scenes, political situations. I remember very well, Bob Cole, who is perhaps the most famous Ghanaian comedian, dramatizing on the stage, during the last days of Nkrumah's rule, the whole business of arresting people, detention camps and so on, with his famous song called 'Aban Kaba' which means 'the government's chains'. The song goes like this: 'When you and I were there, and you saw a policeman following me, did you not know that there was a Government chain on my hands? Now you ask me all kinds of questions, you want to do this to me, you want to do that to me, but you must see that there is a government chain on my hands!' and Bob Cole got away with it because nobody really in the political set-up at that time actually felt that Bob Cole was taking a gibe at the whole Nkrumah structure.

DUERDEN These are the groups that are called concert parties, where you have tours by travelling players who go round singing songs. Perhaps you could say a bit about that yourself?

AWOONOR Yes. These concert parties are quite important. It's interesting that they all began among the Fantis, who have a reputation for being great entertainers. There were groups like the Akan Trio, the Axim Trio, Bob Cole and his concert party, and they toured the country, sort of go on tour for three months or six months, the whole country, with a repertory of plays. These plays are music, mime and dance, and dialogue which is always in Fanti – very witty dialogue and they sort of pick up something from the Minstrel Shows, the Black and White Minstrel Show because they paint themselves white on the face, this is very interesting, and they wear all kinds of clothes, cast-off tail coats and top hats and the women's parts are played by men continuously. Now, these people, any time they came into a village, well in the afternoon, one of them would go about town dressed like a hunchback with a bell and a placard both in front and behind him, and he'd sing to the whole of the town, with a mask on; and when we were kids, we used to follow them right until the evening when the performance was going to start, and literally everybody went to see these concerts. This was the kind of popular entertainment, which, when it came to town and you missed it, you really had missed something. This tradition is still very much alive. As I said, it has become involved in a lot of other things. It has become involved in politics. They sing political songs, perform political plays. They dig gibes at the establishment, and they get away with it because they make people laugh. They make people laugh at themselves, they make people laugh at the government, not in a direct way. They make people feel sad because of certain developments in the society, but essentially, they are comedians.

DUERDEN What sort of counterpart exists of this concert part, in Ghanaian traditional society?

AWOONOR Well, one might say perhaps that all these can be traced back to the traditional music set-up, especially in my own society, among the Ewe. There were, what you call the Halo groups – 'Halo' means songs of abuse, and the Halo groups, I remember, used to be very very powerful, and every village had a group. If a village had a quarrel with another village, a day was appointed, the two groups met, somewhere on neutral ground, and they sang songs of abuse at each other. Now, who produced the best songs, the best songs that were the most effective invective was not really adjudged as such, but the people would decide for themselves and the people would also decide who came off worse in this contest of words and of music. Now and then they led to some kind of civil strife and there was a most idiotic Britisher, a district commissioner, who saw in these groups a source of dissension, a source of conflict, and he banned them, literally drove them underground.

DUERDEN These groups who sing Halo, are they the people who belong to the Commoners' Associations?

AWOONOR Very much so.

DUERDEN The associations of the young men and women?

AWOONOR Yes, very much so. The counterpart of this in the Akan areas is the Asafo companies, which are still very powerful. Asafo is limited very much to the Akan-speaking areas and also to the Northern part of Eweland which has had a lot of contact with the Ashantis. Of course, Asafo in Ashanti is no longer there, simply because of the various wars that they fought with the . . .

DUERDEN These Halo groups. Are they the same as Asafo?

AWOONOR They are very much the same, yes, very much the same pattern as the Asafo. Perhaps without the same organizational structure as the Asafo, because the Asafos are organized essentially as warrior groups; warrior groups of young men, sometimes they run into seven groups or ten groups as the case may be, and they were the king-makers, the chief-makers, they were the fighters, they were the hunters and still, in Winneba which is among the Efutu people, they have a great festival called the deer-hunt festival which falls – I've forgotten exactly when – sometime in August or so, when the Asafos go into the forest, and the first Asafo group which brings in a live deer which will be sacrificed to the God Penkyem Otu is regarded as the winning company of the year and they have a special position in the chief's court and so on. They enjoy certain privileges. Of course their warrior functions have already been dissipated by the coming of colonial administration.

DUERDEN   What I was interested in, in particular, was that you were talking about their having functions for making chiefs.

AWOONOR   Yes.

DUERDEN   How did that work?

AWOONOR   The chiefs are normally what we would call elected leaders. They came from special families of course, but they have to be elected by a council of elders, and the council of elders are also leaders of Asafo groups, and they will have to sit down and decide who will be the best chief. If, after the chief has been elected and he sort of refuses to accept the wishes and directions of his people, the Asafo group will have to meet again, and depose him, that is take the sandals off his feet. Sometimes drive him off into exile, or install another chief. So now and then Asafo companies always normally came to clashes because various Asafo leaders are favoured by their own Asafo companies to become chief, so you always have conflicts developing because this group wants this man to be the chief, the other group wants that man to be chief. And in that condition it is always very difficult. That is why sometimes Asafos can come to blows.

DUERDEN   Yes. But what role does singing play in all this? I mean would you find that a campaign against a chief or against rival candidates would be conducted by songs?

AWOONOR   It would habitually be conducted by songs. And the Asafos are people who are famous for singing war-songs. This is what they sing, for instance: 'Raindrops, we are frightening you. We – it is us. Kweku Nino. There they go, running from our taunts.' And the Asafos, as they come marching into a village, come with their songs and their drums. And before a war is conducted the whole thing is a dramatized situation of music, taunts and shouts. And the Asafo yells are given. I mean this is enough to scare the hell out of anybody. And how powerful the Asafo group is depends upon what good singers they have, what good drummers they have. The people could marshal them with that military enthusiasm which is all part of the musical attachment of these groups to whatever ideas they hold, with which they will fight, frighten the opposition.

DUERDEN   How does the Kinka fit into the Asafo? I mean...

AWOONOR   Yes, I would describe the Kinka, or any other kind of music of the same type as the Kinka, as falling within the umbrella of the bigger structure of the Asafo organization, because the Asafo organization, as I said earlier, has a military orientation, while the Kinka, the Tudzi, Gabada, or any other such musical organization, is in a large sense purely entertaining.

DUERDEN   What's the Tudzi and the Gabada?

AWOONOR   Tudzi and the Gabada are also similar ...

DUERDEN   But in different parts?

AWOONOR   In different parts. They also obtain in Northern Eweland among the Hos and the Pandos. In fact, there was a famous Tudzi group called Bobobo group in Kpandi, which was one of Nkrumah's favourite groups, and he used to have them down – to come down from the hills in Eweland to Accra, to drum for him. And after the military takeover in 1966, they continued to play their music until one day a contingent of soldiers were sent to seize their drums. I mean, they invariably came to a conclusion that it may be possible that they could use the same musical thing to, as it were, sing songs of praises for Nkrumah, which would go against the grain politically in Ghana.

DUERDEN   So the Kinka group is a group of musicians who exist for entertainment purposes only. I mean, what would happen in a war? I mean, would they actually take part as musicians in that case?

AWOONOR   Well, I have explained earlier on, Dennis, that all these groups, as it were, have emerged simply because the militant purposes of the Asafo have vanished.

DUERDEN   So the Kinka is new – is a completely new one?

AWOONOR   Yes, it's a new development, much more sophisticated than the purely traditional patterns of drumming. They use everything, you might even have them using European instruments, but this is very rare. But they use the ordinary Kinka drums, which are like flat boards with hides on them. They put their hands in, and then they have these big boxes with iron railings, which they call the Aziwa, and they play that. All these are instruments that they've had – have sort of emerged because they want to create new things – they didn't want to go back to the old drums, and use the old drums in Kinka, even though one or two drums may be used. They have evolved new instruments, as it were.

DUERDEN   You say they don't want to go back and use the old drums in Kinka?

AWOONOR   Yes, because the old drums are rather cumbersome to carry around.

DUERDEN   I mean, they didn't want to use the old drums that were used by the Asafo musicians?

AWOONOR   By the Asafo musicians, yes. The Kinka has to be mobile, and they have to go through town and drum for everybody. So drums have to be carried, and to have to carry those big long drums, I mean – these are really for settling down and playing for a group around you. But a Kinka is more or less what you might call strolling performers.

DUERDEN   Well now, it seems as if what we call the concert party actually then, sprang out from the same kind of thing.

AWOONOR   Exactly.

DUERDEN   You have the young people getting together and now, instead of being entertained by singing war songs, and getting involved in wars and things, now they are finding other activities . . .

AWOONOR   Yes.

DUERDEN   For themselves . . .

AWOONOR   That's right.

DUERDEN   And forming sort of Kinka groups, in their own villages, but also in the towns forming the concert parties you spoke of?

AWOONOR   Yes, yes, yes – this is very true. A Kinka group may even have attached to it a kind of entertaining, concert little group, but in a very rudimentary sense of the theatre, if one talks about the concert parties as such in terms of theatre. But as I've stressed, they are mainly for entertainment. A Kinka group can be hired by one village, a famous Kinka group will be hired from somewhere to come and play somewhere else at an occasion.

DUERDEN   There's a similar thing in the Ivory Coast, where I believe, people are rather similar to the people in Ghana, and you have a thing called Gumbé, which has been filmed by Jean Rouch, of young men and women in the town getting together . . .

AWOONOR   In fact Gumbé is even played in Ghana in certain parts.

DUERDEN   Where?

AWOONOR   Well, Gumbé, among the sort of Western region Akans you know, who have a lot of affinity with the Ivorians.

DUERDEN   Shall we turn to the Fante songs?

AWOONOR   Yes, well, there is Adenkun, which is similar to the Kinka, very similar. This is the music organization, the musical organization of young people purely for entertainment. And they normally have a girl, who sort of starts the song, and the drums pick it up and everybody joins in. Here they say all kinds of things – they cast aspersions; they give moral stories and so on. As an example, there's this song which in the first verse is saying, 'The devil enemy deceived you – he did it for you – Adua, my father's sister. The devil enemy your relative deceived you – he did it to you. Namama, you left me in solitude. I did not hurt you. It wasn't me. It is the devil enemy, your relative. He did that to you.' And they will go on and on and on, and sing about death, about life, about love. Just as the Kinka groups would do. This is a Fante variant of the Kinka.

DUERDEN Now, in several other societies, not only in West Africa, but for instance, Herskovits has described what happens in Surinam society where the thing came from West Africa, and, by the way, it's extraordinary that in Herskovits's Surinam songs, you get a lot of references to the Ghanaian history of the eighteenth century, which has been preserved there and has not been preserved in Ghana. Now, in Surinam, apparently, the young women can get together and sing songs when, for example, one of their group has committed adultery, or they can go and sing outside her lover's house to bring shame on him. Among the Ibos, the women, when they want one of the women to pay a debt, will go and sing obscene songs outside her house, in order to make her pay up. Do you know, are there similar things amongst your people?

AWOONOR Well, I think the similarity here will be in the Halo structure. The Halo structure, as I said, is organized to bring shame upon other people, either upon a village or upon individuals who have misbehaved. The Halo refer to them by name, abuse them, and they get away with it, because there is a free licence that the other person who is being abused can also organize a rival group, if he can, to do the same thing to the leaders of the rival Halo group. And I think this sounds to me something rather similar to what you mentioned as obtaining in Surinam. But whether they're going to get to the details of being involved with a woman who's committed adultery, and going to her house, and insulting her and so on – I don't know of any example in recent years. What I do know is that in our society which is polygamous, in the wide sense of the word, rival wives do have songs – do compose songs, which they sing against their rivals. They may not be addressing them directly. For example, a woman who's had a quarrel with her rival, she sees a hen passing, and she says to the hen, 'Look at this!' I mean, the hen comes to eat her food, or something, she sort of drives the hen away and says 'Look at her legs like broomsticks!' or something similarly scathing. And, of course, she's referring to her rival.

Well, you have this thing, this is a kind of verbal interplay and counterplay; one glimpses the verbal inventiveness of the languages in which they use these things. And the use of irony and sarcasm are all part of it.

DUERDEN It's been said by people that this is a way of getting rid of all kinds of conflicts: by actually singing about it, you sort of verbalize the conflict, and you dissipate it.

AWOONOR Well, as the performer or the musician does this sort of thing in public, everybody knows what he's talking about, and everybody laughs, everybody enjoys it, so it's no longer interesting – it's no longer important for the conflict to, as it were, be reduced to physical terms where people are going to be at each other's throats. And this, I think, is a good escape valve in African societies.

DUERDEN So your District Commissioner, who was suppressing the Halo groups, when they were singing for rival villages was, in fact, perhaps making the conflicts worse.

AWOONOR Exactly. I mean, he didn't understand anything about what was going on. I mean, he thought when people met in village squares and sang songs at each other, the next thing was that they were going to take up cudgels; they never did. If they were going to use cudgels at all, they would have taken up cudgels in the first place. They didn't need songs to take cudgels for them. As you said, very correctly, songs, as it were, will dramatize the conflict, and therefore make it unnecessary for any physical conflict to be initiated by any side at all. If you felt too hurt about what your rival had said, you could go and compose a better, and a much more strongly-worded, song, which would put him to shame. Well today, as I said earlier, the Asafo still is very much in evidence, especially among the Fantis; where the Asafo is very well organized in Cape Coast, in Elmina, in Winneba and they are part of the modern structure, they take part in community self-help projects, but their music, their songs, their war songs are still there. If they're going to build a village pit latrine, for example, they march with a song to go and build a village pit latrine; this is the direction of their energies, which now I consider as a very colourful aspect of the life of the people. They go for this great festival, of the Efutu people, which comes on, and this is a spectacle which goes on from dawn till evening, and the Asafos go into the forest to catch deer with bare hands. And as they come into town, the first thing you hear is their song – and these are war songs, which in the olden days would be directed against an enemy, but now, of course, there is this healthy rivalry, an almost sportive spirit of competition, geared around a religious ceremony of catching deer – which would later be sacrificed to the god – which brought them to that area.

DUERDEN One thing I wanted to ask you about was what about the part played by Asafo or Halo in local government?

AWOONOR Well, yes, Asafo and Halo are very much part of the local government structure. Groups invariably emerge which may not agree with a particular District Commissioner. Then there will be musicians who perform, who, without actually calling his name directly, dramatize the stupidity of that particular man in songs. This, as it were, was a way of bringing up people's political emotions into the open by providing a venue, providing a channel for social self-expression via the musicians who would say, 'Look, here we have this man whom we know – his grandfather was a goat thief, it's remembered he stole goats, and he's now the man who is coming to lord it over us in this area, isn't it a shame!'

DUERDEN — But to return to the traditional application of the music: these songs would be used in what kind of wars? I mean between villages or —

AWOONOR Yes, they would be used between villages, they would be used between tribes in the olden days. They did form a very great part of the Ashanti war structure, before they were suppressed by the British. They were in fact the spearhead of the whole Ashanti war organization.

Even among the Anlos, my own people, the Asafo wings, what they call the Asafo wings, are real war wings. You had the Dusi, which was a right wing, the Mia which was a left wing, and Dome which was a middle 'wing', the central body. They always had a three-pronged formation in this way. And each Asafo group knew where they would go if a war broke out. If the Anlos were attacked, they always had a place called Asadame where they all gathered and they moved on the enemy in that formation.

DUERDEN All the young men joined these Asafo associations when they reached manhood presumably. And there were initiation ceremonies, weren't there?

AWOONOR Yes. There were initiation ceremonies. When you came of age, the first thing your father did for you was to buy you a gun, the symbol of manhood, and the next thing was to see that a house was built for you. And the next thing was to see that you were initiated into an Asafo group. And the Asafo group which you joined was invariably the Asafo group of your own father, the group he belonged to when he was a young man. And you carried on from there. That was the tradition. Your children would join the same Asafo group.

When the military functions of the Asafos became obsolete in modern times, the Asafo became much more what you might call voluntary associations, in which young people gathered together, did work on community self-help projects and what not.

DUERDEN How were the drummers and musicians chosen?

AWOONOR The drummers and the musicians normally were what you might call traditional drummers and musicians. There were special families who had the gift of music, had the gift of song, had the gift of drums. And they provided the drummers and the musicians. If they were going to war their function mainly was just to drum for the Asafo army, to fight on with.

DUERDEN Who actually invented the songs?

AWOONOR Well, the musicians and the drummers invented their own songs within the context of the Asafo temperament, the Asafo's feeling, the Asafo's emotions, which they were part and parcel of. They were what you might call the poets and the dramatists of the Asafo groups.

DUERDEN   Did they have cult gods?

AWOONOR   The Asafos normally would have what you might call cult gods, but they were all – you might say – part and parcel of one particular religion or the other. I gave an example of the Winneba, the Penkyem Otu god, which is the ancestral god which brought them to this place. So every religious ceremony of the Asafos was based on Penkyem Otu. And only the specific form of ritual would vary from place to place.

DUERDEN   What about the musicians and the drummers? I mean would they have gods of their own?

AWOONOR   Yes. Among the Ewes – I don't know very much about the Akans – but among the Ewes we had, have still, what you call Hadzi voodoo, which was the God of Songs. A man sang because he had a God of Songs: it was created for him by the shrine, by the household god, around whom he had his being and moved. And he had to perform certain ceremonies, he had to erect a little shrine for his God of Songs. And if a day came and he had to perform and he went and poured libations and the divination told him not to sing that day he had to agree, because his God of Songs was not in any mood, you know, to sing.

DUERDEN   And when he was doing particularly well would it be that he was possessed by the God?

AWOONOR   Yes, there's always, there were always the ceremonies or the periods of possession; these, of course, were limited to certain cults, for example, to the Yewe cult, also to the Dente and what you call the medicine cults. The medicine cults were the cults of healers, traditional healers, who had knowledge of herbs and were in communion with the gods, and therefore in a performance when they were singing they could, as it were, be translated into somebody else. They became not-part-of-this-world; they became the god himself who had descended into and through them. And they went through a frenzied period of identification with that god. This, of course, would last for a short while. Then they were back among the living.

DUERDEN   What was the Yewe cult?

AWOONOR   The Yewe cult is the cult of thunder, which is still very powerful among the Anlos. It is, apart from the Klama cult of the Krobos, perhaps one of the most well-organized cults in West Africa. They had quite a few cults also in Western Nigeria, one hears. But the Yewe cult is the cult of thunder worshippers. Children are taken at the age of 10, 12, and they are sent into a chosen place, they live there, they get initiated and they take new names, they wear the cross, what we call the dakpla of the god, which is the mark on their back. And when they come out, nobody who is not a cult member can call them by their own names because if they do, they offend the god. And they have all kinds of drums: they have a slow Yewe drum, they have a fast-beating Yewe drum. When the god of thunder sort of descends, they have the day of killing the rams, and that day really is the culmination of the whole period of initiation. They do it once a year. They have the magicians who perform in public and so on and so forth.

DUERDEN How would these cults exist in relationship to these young men's associations we were talking about? Presumably these are separate?

AWOONOR No, they are not invariably, they are not too distinct and separate. The cults, you might say, are, the membership of the cult is voluntary, but you can be selected by the gods. If you were ill and your father took you to Fetish and the divinations were made, you would be told that you did not give a son – that is, your father would be told that he did not give a son to Yewe. So one of his children, a daughter or a son, would have to go into Yewe. This in its way is the link between the Asafo and the cults themselves. But the cults do not have any open thing to do with the Asafo groups. The Asafo members can be members of the cults, but invariably their membership of the cult, which is a secret organization, is not expected to be trumpeted in the open in terms of the Asafo's open activities.

DUERDEN Yes. In the actual expression of the Asafo there wouldn't be any reference to the cults?

AWOONOR No, no.

DUERDEN But what about these musicians and singers and so on, who you say have a cult, do they have a god of their own.

AWOONOR Yes. These are what you might call personal gods. The musician, a musician's family will definitely have a personal god, what are called the Hadzi voodoo. In that family of singers or drummers, there is a little shrine somewhere to which they go, they perform the ceremonies before they come out into the open and drum or sing. And when the god descends upon them in public, everybody knows that it is not they who are singing, it is their Hadzi voodoo who is right there with them by their side. And he is telling them to say the sort of things that they are singing.

DUERDEN So, he may be responsible for their producing new songs?

AWOONOR Yes. He may be responsible for their producing new songs. In fact I remember I did a poem some years ago called 'My God of Songs was Ill': 'I had to cross a river with my God of Songs because he was ill.

And when I went to this shrine they said I should come in with my backside; because of my God of Song being ill I could not sing any more. I just couldn't sing until there was this rapport between myself and my god. It is only then that I can sing.' That is a paraphrase of 'My God of Songs was Ill'.*

DUERDEN   Is this a translation of something traditional . . . ?

AWOONOR   No, not a translation of a traditional song, but it is the translation of a traditional idea, in terms of the musician or the poet's relationship with his god. And I noticed Christopher Okigbo expressing almost the same thing which I read the other day in one of the transcripts of your Transcription Centre interviews where he says, 'When I write a poem, it's not me writing it, you know. When I create the drum beats it is not me: it is the drums that create these things. I am just an instrument.'† And this is exactly what I am saying.

DUERDEN   Were you aware of this kind of thing in your own childhood?

AWOONOR   Oh yes. I was very much part and parcel of my mother's family, which was involved in the Yewe thing, even though I wasn't a member. My grandfather had a compound, what you call a Yewe compound. And we had a fetish hut – we still have it. My uncle who is now the Regent, as it were, the Stool, is a fetish priest. And he, right in his second bedroom, had what you call the Afa. The Afa oracle, which is analogous, and the word itself probably cognate, with the Yoruba 'Ifa' or oracle. The Ewes came from Nigeria, as it were, and they have a lot to do with the Yorubas. They have a lot of affinity with the Yorubas and the Dahomeans. They, in fact our languages, can be slightly inter-intelligible to each other, especially Ewe and Fon. As I was saying about my uncle, he is very much in the centre of this kind of cult life.

DUERDEN   But what about these young men's associations? Were you sort of introduced to them or . . . ?

AWOONOR   No, I wasn't. I wasn't introduced to them because I left rather early, being torn away by my father who wanted us to go to school. I mean there was no nonsense about this. And then you didn't have anything to do with it. Of course, going to a missionary school if you were seen even witnessing Yewe drums, I mean you were given a hell of a beating the next day, in school. And of course my father himself not being a Christian didn't care very much whether you went to see Yewe or not. But you were part of a missionary educational system, so you wouldn't dare. So one lost

---

* Cf. *Rediscovery and other poems* – George Awoonor Williams (Mbari, Ibadan, 1964), p. 31.
† Cf. Serumaga interview with Okigbo, this volume, p. 143.

touch. But we always went back in the holidays and so on, and you became part of it distantly because we lived in a household which was very much involved in it. I remember my mother used to belong to an Oleke drumming group years ago when I was a little boy, and I used to go with her.

DUERDEN   What was an Oleke drumming group?

AWOONOR   Well Oleke is what you might call the lovers' drumming group in which young girls and young men drummed, and they had all kinds of flirtatious dances and songs. But this was purely for entertainment, and my mother was one of the leaders in this group. This was years ago, you know, Dennis.

Dennis Brutus
BORN 1924

▼▼▼▼▼▼▼▼▼▼▼▼▼▼▼▼▼▼▼▼▼▼▼▼▼▼▼▼

When Dennis Brutus was interviewed by Cosmo Pieterse in October 1966, he had just arrived in England after his release from a South African jail.

His first collection of poems, *Sirens Knuckles Boots* had been published in 1963 by Mbari; he had written all the poems which he and Pieterse were to collect into the volume *Letters to Martha*, published by Heinemann, London, 1968. Three further selections from his poetry have since appeared under Brutus's name, two published by American universities and non-commercially circulated: the *Denver Poems* published in 1969 by the University of Denver, and *Poems from Algiers*, 1970, the second occasional publication of the African and Afro-American Research Institute, The University of Texas at Austin. The third work is a selection of poems spanning the years 1961–1969 in *Seven South African Poets*, edited by Cosmo Pieterse and published by Heinemann, London, in 1971.

Dennis Brutus is now working on a collected edition of his own poetry, and on a selection of the work of Arthur Nortje, an ex-student of his, who died in December 1970.

PIETERSE   This afternoon in the studio of the Transcription Centre, we have Dennis Brutus, the South African poet, educationalist, sportsman and politician; we are having an interview with him, mainly about his poetic work. To start the interview we would like to ask Dennis to read one of the poems from his collection *Sirens Knuckles Boots*. Dennis, could you please read for us the introductory poem to your volume.

BRUTUS   'A troubadour, I traverse all my land
exploring all her wide flung parts with zest
probing in motion sweeter far than rest
her secret thickets with an amorous hand:

and I have laughed disdaining those who banned
enquiry and movement, delighting in the test

of wills when doomed by Saracened arrest,
choosing, like unarmed thumb, simply to stand.

Thus quixoting till a cast-off of my land,
I sing and fare, person to loved-one pressed
braced for this pressure and the captor's hand
that snaps off service like a weathered strand:
no mistress favour has adorned my breast
only the shadow of an arrow-brand.'

PIETERSE Thank you, Dennis. Well, one notices in poems of yours that fairly frequently there are these opposites for instance, here 'exploring all her wide flung parts with zest | probing in motion sweeter far than rest' – now, take 'motion' and its antithesis 'rest'; is this a feature, an element of your poetry that you consciously strive after, or does this come out of, can one call it an inner philosophic meaning that is behind your life, behind your work; something perhaps unconscious? Is this something you do quite consciously?

BRUTUS A very large question I'm afraid and I must start off by saying that I hadn't noticed that particular contrast. I think it is true to say that in my work there is a tension and this tension is partly a deliberate desire to catch tension, because I think tension is of the essence of good poetry. On the other hand, I think the circumstances in which I, and most South Africans live, is one which creates tensions, so I suppose the answer is partly that it is a deliberate choice and partly it's an expression of temperament.

PIETERSE Temperament, choice, and you said the circumstances of the country. Would there be a philosophy that you subscribe to, a philosophy that deals in terms of tensions; some kind of dialectic perhaps that is expounded in your verse?

BRUTUS A question like that could have a number of answers, each, I think, dealing with a different aspect or facet of South African life. The image, for instance, of a thumb, an upturned thumb, is in fact deliberately drawn from the salute of the African Congress, which at one stage was a thumbs-up signal.

PIETERSE Could I also just interpose here and ask whether this could also be the troubadour who is hiking, who is hitching?

BRUTUS Yes, indeed, although I think you are giving my work a depth that it doesn't really deserve. But just in the previous line the reference to 'Saracen', which is to me related at once to the Middle Ages, the Crusades in fact, and the conflict between Crusader and Saracen (one thinks immediately of Saladin or Sala-u-din) and, on the other hand, the use of 'Saracens' as armoured cars by the South African police – they were imported from Britain; we nicknamed them 'Skerpioene' or 'Scorpions'. But there is a deliberate attempt there to play on both the Saracen in a medieval context and the modern Saracen as the armoured car of the South African police.

PIETERSE   I see, thank you. I noticed for instance you have the word 'quixoting' which one would normally think of as a proper noun, doing duty as a verb. And very often composites like 'mistress-favour'. Could you comment on these?

BRUTUS   Yes, I don't know how far they will illuminate my work broadly; the poem is a special one, I think. But Don Quixote is to me a variation on the troubadour idea. The man who goes 'tilting with wind-mills' is not very much different from the troubadour, minstrel or el trovatore – I think this is the same thing – the man who travelled across Europe, fighting and loving and singing. It's the combination of conflict and music in the troubadour which interests me – the man who can be both fighter and poet, and this is a kind of contradiction which is also present in Don Quixote.

PIETERSE   For a moment, could we just dwell on this point; Don Quixote 'tilts at windmills', is a romantic, and to some extent, shall we say, a blind fighter. To what extent do you feel this would be true about the fight that goes on in your poetry? The struggle that you wage so, it seems to me, strongly and physically. I don't see anything of Don Quixote in you?

BRUTUS   Well, I don't know what you do see. May I try and answer the question by saying, and I don't want to complicate it too much, I would say there are three answers here. There is a political struggle in South Africa; there is my personal conflict, which eventually brought me to prison, with the apartheid regime; and then there is, as you point out, the conflict, the tension in the poetry itself. Now I think it is true, and at least one person writing in *Transition* about my work said this,* that there is an element of laughter in my work; it may be that I am engaged in a fight but at the same time I find a certain delight in it. I enjoy the fight; and this is where the laughter and the music, the gaiety and the humour come in. I can laugh at myself and see myself as a little like Don Quixote, tilting at windmills or, if you like, fighting a losing battle.

PIETERSE   I'd like to say that I think you do yourself an injustice – not a losing battle, certainly that is not the tenor, the resonance of your verse. There is zest in it – there's a kind of strength in it, which I find again very often expressed in your linking the physical, the human body, with the physical of nature. Soul and soil are very often transmuted, fused together.

* *Transition*, Vol. 5, No. (iv), 1965.

Could you comment on this? Have I read you correctly or am I going up a wrong path altogether?

BRUTUS   I think you've summed up very aptly and neatly when you say 'soul and soil'. I do think that although I haven't put it in those exact terms I do have that in mind. When I speak of South Africa as a mistress then it is both woman and country – there is no doubt about that. So it is in fact a physical body if you like – a physical presence in the sense of flesh. At the same time it is the land I traverse. I do not know whether we should confine ourselves to this particular poem, but when I say something to the effect of 'pressed to the loved one in an intimate contact', this is the kind of image one would use of a sexual embrace. But it is also what I deliberately used, the same image as indicating contact with the earth. And then the reference you made earlier to 'Mistress-favour'. What I am trying to say is that my loyalty has not been to any woman in the sense that the troubadours or knights of chivalry wore a particular woman's favour. For me the favour has been instead the knowledge which I predicted in the poem – the knowledge that I would eventually end in prison; because the arrow-brand at the end is the image readily acceptable in Britain: it used to be the standard symbol of a convict in prison – the uniform with arrows on. So what I end by saying is that instead of being loyal to a particular woman, my loyalty has been to the country with the shadow of an arrow constantly over me – this would be my mistress's favour.

PIETERSE   From what you've said, although I know we've just been touching the surface, and from some of my readings of your poetry, it seems that there are very many meanings locked into single words, into single lines, and certainly innumerable meanings in a whole poem. I want to ask two questions about this. The first, are there any influences of which you are aware, influences from the poetic field, that have been introduced into, or let's rather say, have been absorbed into your own poetry?

BRUTUS   Yes. Was that the one question? Well certainly during my years at University, and since then as well, one of the principal poets in terms of approach to poetry, the principal influence, has been John Donne. And in fact all the metaphysicals have a very strong appeal for me. I have, too, been influenced to some extent, I think, by my repeated readings of Eliot, of Yeats, and possibly because I read him at a very impressionable age, the writings of James Joyce – and very particularly, I suppose, *Ulysses* – influenced me.

PIETERSE   I seem to feel also that you are doing what Shelley advised Keats to do, loading 'every rift with ore'. There's a Keatsian quality in your poetry too. And the second question is this. All these many meanings – do they not make the poetry too complex, too rich, do they not stand between the reader and poem?

BRUTUS   Well, I'm glad you asked that question because it's one I've often asked myself and to which I have given an answer which seems very unpopular with my current readers. Ever since I came out of Robben Island I've been trying to work towards a very much greater simplicity in my work, and this is partly because I answered your question in the affirmative. I felt my work was too clotted, too thick, there were too many strands knotted together, I was trying to make the language do too many things at the same time. And so I've turned to a very much simpler, very prosaic use of the language and almost everybody who's read my later poetry is convinced that it is far inferior to the early poetry!

PIETERSE   Dennis, that is very interesting, could we pursue it a bit later but at this stage I'd like to interject this question. Your earlier poetry, was it intended for a certain kind of audience – say a literary-conscious audience, or did you have the man in the pub, perhaps, the man in the street, the man at home, or the pupils and the student in the school, did you have people like this in mind? The less mature reader.

BRUTUS   Well, it isn't easy to answer. If I say that every poem in *Sirens Knuckles Boots* was written for a particular person or to serve a particular function and that not one of these poems was written with an audience in mind, this will partly answer the question. I was, in fact, writing letters to particular people in the form of a poem, or making a point that I had failed to make in a conversation, but not one of them was written for publication, and not one of them was written with an audience in mind.

PIETERSE   May I interject again. How did the publication of these poems come about?

BRUTUS   Very interesting. Some of my work got into the hands of Ulli Beier, who at that time was preparing a Penguin anthology, and he wrote to me expressing regret that the work had reached him too late for use in the anthology;* but he suggested that if I sent some more it could be turned into a book. So I scratched around for stuff, some of it was ten or fifteen years old, and whatever I could find – and much of my stuff, I suppose about 80 per cent, is lost, in fact – but what I could find I sent him, and the book came out while I was in prison and I was in fact interrogated about it and a further charge would have been brought against me, except that I quite honestly couldn't remember the date at which I had

---

* Some of Brutus's work is, in fact, in the revised and enlarged 1968 Penguin new edition of Ulli Beier and Gerald Moore's *Modern Poetry from Africa*.

sent these poems off. And if they could have fixed a date I think I would have been prosecuted.

PIETERSE   I see. Would that have been just for writing and getting published, or for a strong political tendency in the poetry?

BRUTUS   No, I think once one is banned, it doesn't matter what you write. As I said to a group in Stratford-on-Avon, last Saturday night, even if you wrote a ballad to your mistress's eyebrow, you'd still end up in 'chookie' (in prison). It didn't matter what you wrote about really, the substance doesn't matter, once you are banned anything you write is by law unpublishable. And so my poetry, post-Robben Island, has in fact had to be in the form of letters, again to people; it was illegal to write poetry, but it was legal to write letters.

PIETERSE   Your post-Robben Island poetry, did you have an audience in mind here? Were the things that you have done subsequent to being released more political than before. The simplification, what was the point of that? What was the purpose you were pursuing?

BRUTUS   Well, most of it is addressed to an individual – my sister-in-law in fact. My brother is in prison and I wrote to her in the form of letters largely about prison conditions, but I had hoped that they would ultimately reach a wider audience and this may be one reason why I tried and still try to pare my thought down to a very simple basic sort of structure. I'm not sure that's the only reason – I think in prison I also did a lot of rethinking about technique and expression and that is one of the things that persuaded me to seek a simpler idiom. And then, of course, if one is writing as I would be principally for the people of my own continent, and particularly those who are just becoming familiar with the English language – but who one hopes will develop a great love for the language, because it is a fine vehicle for poetry – I think then one must avoid embroidery or anything that would be an interference in, and a barrier against communication between writer and listener.

PIETERSE   From technique to themes. You said most of the poetry you've been writing recently is mainly for an African audience, or about African themes. What particularly would these themes be? The landscape, the geography of the country, if one can put it that way, the beauty of the country, political themes, as one seems to feel that they are mainly in *Sirens Knuckles Boots*, political themes closely wedded to personal themes. Any new ground that you have broken?

BRUTUS   Well, I think the emphasis has changed. In *Sirens* and all the poetry I've written, up to the middle sixties – pre-prison, shall we say – it's lyrical, and it is really love poetry, except that it's not for a woman, but for a country. Since then, it's not so much that my affection has changed, but the emphasis of the affection has changed, more to a statement of what is ugly I think, of what is . . .

PIETERSE   When you say what is ugly; what is ugly in political, social and largely cultural manifestations on the continent, is that what you mean?

BRUTUS   Yes. Well not on the continent so much as a little, narrowly confined to South Africa. I find it harder to say what I am writing about now, than what I used to write about; perhaps if I was at a further remove it would be easier. I would say that for the time being, well for the past year, I have been writing about the political, social conditions, and in a sense condemning them, but not as a politician would condemn them but as a poet who is really just a sensitive and articulate human being.

PIETERSE   Dennis, one thing that strikes me is that you are a man with many interests, poetry apart. You are an educationalist, deeply interested in sports, administration and participation, you are a thinker, you are a politician, and yet one finds that say, for instance, the sportsman, the athlete, doesn't ever come into your poetry. Is there any particular reason?

BRUTUS   Yes, you are right. I am not sure of the reason but I agree with you completely that there are whole areas of my life which seem to be shut out of my poetry; it may just be that they don't make good poetic material.

PIETERSE   Do you think that could be true? Is there anything that doesn't make good poetic material?

BRUTUS   No. Yes. This is what I would say, that you are quite right, so I'm not really serious, this is just a suggestion I threw out. That it's possible they aren't good poetic materials. Alternatively they may not be so integral to my emotional reactions that they are thrown out as images when I am writing poetry. I don't know. I would say, however, that to me the troubadour is not so far from the sportsman – the kind of man who can conduct a fight but not lose his sense of humour or his sense of balance about it is not so far from the gymnast or the athlete who is doing the pole vault. Basically I don't think they are so different in temperament or in character. That I don't use the images of sport is to me even odd, but I can't explain it.

PIETERSE   Could we go on to something completely different. Your impression of the South African poetic scene. What do you think is happening there in terms of perhaps, techniques, themes; are South Africans shut out from poetry, or large areas of poetry perhaps, more personal poetry? Or is there very much personal poetry being written?

BRUTUS   Well, I can only go really by either published poetry or the little bit I have seen in manuscript. There's a great deal of published poetry in South Africa, and a great deal of this is merely third rate or worse. And I've tried to explain why there's this outpouring of what is really a trashy kind of lyrical poetry. I think you find it in things like *Contrast*, you certainly find it in Guy Butler's poetry broadsheet which you may know, which is called *New Coin*, which consists entirely of previously unpublished poetry. Much of this is simply trashy.

PIETERSE I'm sorry, could I interrupt? When you say lyrical outbursts, could you define?

BRUTUS Well they are short, there is no attempt at an epic or a narrative treatment, and they are descriptive of persons or places, or emotions or ideas. To me this is roughly lyrical, and they seem to be so appallingy lacking in substance.

PIETERSE The substance that is lacking, is it because the poets don't deal with things of wide social meaning? They have no social significance? Or is it because they are, as poems, just weak? They have nothing new to say about the things they are talking about?

BRUTUS I think they are simply weak as poems, but, and this is not unrelated to the first part, I don't think the two facets are opposed to each other. I would say that their failure is basically, this is my explanation, their failure basically is there because of a failure to confront life. It is because they don't want to react to the broader situation, either in terms of South Africa or much wider, and this failure, this inhibition, this failure to respond, I think, is what eviscerates the poems and makes them gutless.

PIETERSE Probably our last question, Dennis. Wouldn't, if one expects the poets in South Africa to write mainly about public themes, wouldn't this make them propagandists rather than poets?

BRUTUS Well, perhaps I should just go on and refer briefly to some of the unpublished stuff. I have in mind very particularly a young man who is at present studying at Oxford who is a non-white South African and he seems to be quite the best poet in South Africa today, easily the best. Now Nortje* hasn't been published and much of Nortje's stuff has the same kind of timidity that the published poems of white South Africans exhibit. When I talk of published poetry, as far as I know, one hundred per cent is the poetry of White South Africans, there is little in *Contrast*, or elsewhere, of non-white South Africans.

PIETERSE Now this timidity, what is the precise quality of his timidity?

* Kenneth Arthur Nortje (b. 1942, South Africa, died 1970, Oxford, U.K. while studying for a B.Litt. degree at Jesus College where he had, 1965 to 1967, successfully read for a degree in English), whose poetry first appeared in book form in the new, enlarged and revised (1968) edition of the Beier-Moore Penguin *Modern Poetry from Africa*. A larger selection of his work is to be found in *Seven South African Poets*, (Heinemann, London, 1971). Dennis Brutus is now collecting his poetry for a collection in African Writers Series.

Dennis Brutus

It seems to me from the things of Nortje that I've read that he takes a theme, he takes a particular subject, and he looks at it sharply, he looks at it newly, he cuts through the matter and he gives Nortje's vision of whatever he is talking about. Would that be timidity?

BRUTUS No, on the contrary, I would say this is a very clear indication of a tremendous willingness to grapple with reality, but I want to say that only in half a dozen of Nortje's poems have I seen him at the full stretch of his power. I have seen him on occasions, particularly in two or three of his latest poems, I've seen what his potential really is, as far as I can judge it. And then I think he's tremendously good, I think he's head and shoulders above anybody else in South Africa.

J. P. Clark
BORN 1935

At the time of recording this interview with Lewis Nkosi in September 1962, J. P. Clark had published with Mbari one of his plays *Song of a Goat* and *Poems*. He had also appeared in magazines and anthologies. Later books to appear: *Three Plays* (OUP, 1964) including *Song of a Goat*, *The Masquerade*, and *The Raft;* *America Their America* (Deutsch, 1964) – a book of impressions of America gained there during a visit; *A Reed in the Tide* (Longman, 1965) – a selection of poems from magazines and from the Mbari *Poems*; *Ozidi* (OUP, 1966), an epic play based on the Ijaw saga of Ozidi, told in seven days to dance, music, and mime, and *Casualties* (Longman, 1970), poems written between 1966 and 1968. A collection of Clark's critical essays was published by Longman in 1971 under the title *The Example of Shakespeare*.

NKOSI   Well, J. P. Clark, as one of the leading Nigerian writers I wonder if you could just tell us what set you off on this path – writing.

CLARK   I just felt like writing that's all.

NKOSI   Yes, but how did you begin really, was there some strange incentive which caused you to begin to write?

CLARK   I don't remember any. I really don't. I just feel like writing and I write, you see.

NKOSI   Yes. How long ago did you start writing?

CLARK   Well, it's about six–seven years back.

NKOSI   Of the published works or produced plays, which one of these did you find most difficult?

CLARK   Well, I've written one play so far which is the one that has been performed and published. Well there was a long period of gestation at first, you know, but once I really started writing it wasn't more than a week or so, of actual writing and after that, a couple of days touching up one or two places. But it wasn't more than a week or so, about a week if I can remember correctly.

NKOSI   What is the name of this play?

CLARK   *Song of a Goat*.

NKOSI   Could you tell us something about it – what was it all about?

CLARK   Well, simply, the story to it is – a fisherman, who is a part-time pilot in one of the creeks down the Niger, loses his sexual powers, abilities, and sends his wife for the birth cure. He doesn't want to admit the fault is his and so she goes for the birth cure. The doctor, who is something of a prophet too and a priest, suggests there's no cure, there is nothing the matter with the woman: all the trouble is with the man. The best cure would be for the man to make her over to someone in the family. The two of them, man and wife, don't take to this, but things do tend in this direction: she and the man's younger brother fall for each other, and then there's tragedy: there's resistance from the husband. And that's the story to it really.

NKOSI   Tell me, J.P., there are people who have suggested that you might have been influenced by some modern European playwrights. Have you read any of them and do you find that you've been influenced by people like Ionesco at all?

CLARK   Well, I'd rather say that I may have been influenced by the ancients, the ancient Greeks. They've mentioned Sophocles, and mentioned Euripides, and all that ... I mean, this is in the use of myth and what appears to the critics as myth and the use of poetry as the vehicle, as the language vehicle and I suppose we've been led on to believe that my work is derived from the Greek classics because I use the chorus and I use one or two other things which people imagine are the exclusive qualities of Greek tragedy. And in this connection we have mentioned, also, a modern T. S. Eliot and it's said that I have used the same medium as he uses in his *Murder in the Cathedral* for instance. In this case if there is any modern influence at all may be it is that.

NKOSI   I've also wondered about other things as far as Nigerian writers are concerned. There's a very rich theatrical tradition, I'm told, even in theatrical forms. Do you find that you have yourself the desire to borrow from these forms or to improve upon them?

CLARK   Yes, if there was any preoccupation at all during the writing of this play, it was with the burial rites in my place, the burial rites of the Ijaws, of the Niger Delta. Now, in these rituals, I mean, there is Greek drama, and then there is an Ijaw drama too and it is embedded in this ritual. I find it most compelling in the use of a leader, the use of the chorus, mime and dancing, the use of song; and the whole enactment is simply – is really complicated but it has a rigid line which is known by everybody from the youngest child to the oldest wise-man, from the oldest grey grandmother to the youngest capable of participation. I think there is here this cultural coincidence. I rather believe that people like Yeats are right who say that at bottom all people are the same, all folklores, mythologies, spring from the same sources.

NKOSI   Yes, and following from this, J.P., do you find that the Nigerian audiences respond to these theatrical forms whilst they are remote from their traditional context for instance when you have transformed them into some kind of foreign theatrical vehicle like in the idea of the western-type play which you are using?

CLARK   Of course, Nigeria is a very large place with lots of different people. I can only speak for my section of the country and as I have said, we have these tremendous rituals which I think can stand and have many things in common with Greek tragedy as I have said; and even on the comedy side, on the lighter side there is the bridal ritual, for instance, when a girl undergoes the circumcision rite and out from there to the husband's house. It follows a set pattern and there are all sorts of things done and I mean this contains big possibilities for theatre development. But the time comes when you do use this type of material: you apply a story to it, and then you apply the English language to it – you've got to express it artistically and I express myself on the literary level in the English language. By this time you do actually also see the degradation from the origin of whatever material you are using; you see, by the time you finish with it, people may not recognize what, maybe, was common to everybody before.

NKOSI   Do you yourself write with any kind of audience in mind?

CLARK   I have tried very much to – I believe in communication, I believe you must get to as many people as you can. I suppose for over a year I laid off from writing what I call chamber poetry, that is the occasional piece. You see, I believed this was a bit snobbish, esoteric, you know, and I thought the thing that can really get in to everybody, however different in background or in upbringing, is what can be put on the stage. I mean this is not a question of what type of stage now, but I believe this is the type of thing that you can go to, all sorts of people can go to and then each man gets what he can out of it.

NKOSI   Well, I'm certainly interested in this because you seem to differ from another Nigerian poet, Christopher Okigbo, who seems to think that the function of the poet or writer is to concern himself exclusively with art even to the point of excluding those who might not appreciate it as much as other professional writers appreciate it,* so he would suggest that poets should write for other poets, for an exclusive mutual admiration club.

* Cf. *Transition*, Vol. 2, No. 5, July/Aug. 1962, on 'Writers' Conference, and interview with Okigbo', p. 192.

CLARK   No, I remember in East Africa during the conference,* you remember you were there, you see. Chris did rub people the wrong way when he said, 'Oh! I read my poems only to poets', and all that. I think that was either just some stage reaction or something like that, really. I mean, a gauging-the-audience reaction type of remark, because if there is anybody I have worked with very closely – I have stayed with him when I was at the University College at Ibadan, and he was working as a teacher – in fact, if there was any one great champion of my own poetry, it was Chris. And I can say this – that I started him off in his writing; and we've discussed these things together, we've thought of writing manifestos several times, and we hold many beliefs which we have thrown overboard several times only to make new ones. I think Chris was just being contrary.

NKOSI   No. I'm not referring in particular to what he said at Kampala,* but I think that Chris would agree that this is one of his attitudes to audiences or to readers who might want to approach his work but in fact he is indifferent to how they react to it, that is what he said to me.

CLARK   Well, I think this is a front: I don't think he really means it. I think he is taken too seriously, for example, if he wants to write a novel, he has already got plans, he's been working on a novel, a trilogy, you see. He really wants to get to people; the other face is a front. There is no doubt that one of the things we said we believed, which we took, I suppose, from Eliot, was that good poetry must be difficult. You just can't go and pluck it like a rose or something like that and then sniff at it and that's that . . . I mean there is more to good poetry than mere surface . . . you must make some effort for the reader to get what really is there, so that when we use imagery that some people find too personal or too remote we say they must make some effort to penetrate to the meaning, through the mood and the music . . . and I suppose the general public don't want to – they want things cut and dried. It is in that aspect he says he writes for people who care enough to make the effort to understand.

NKOSI   Yes, now tell me about these writers, the young Nigerian writers. Do the writers in general in Nigeria form a sort of a common movement around Mbari or what is your attitude towards each other?

CLARK   Well, as I said, I worked closely with Christopher Okigbo for instance, and then there's Wole Soyinka: you know we went to the same schools, as it were, we went to the same university, most of us: Chinua Achebe, for instance, Wole Soyinka, Christopher Okigbo, we all went to the same university and we work in the same towns and we go to the same places as it were, we talk a lot among ourselves but we don't present a

* Cf. *Transition*, Vol. 2, No. 5, July/Aug. 1962, on 'Writers' Conference, and interview with Okigbo', p. 192.

front. All we ask is that there are certain standards which are accepted in most places, you see where this type of art is either practised or enjoyed, and these criteria must be upheld, and if you are going to break them you must have something really good and original to offer to convince people that these things are outdated. In other words, people must have the necessary educational background. This is all we ask as a united front, I suppose.

NKOSI Now about your plans: are you working on anything, and what are you planning to do in the near future?

CLARK I'm going on to Princeton in America right now and I've asked to be away for a year or so but within that time, I expect I'll finish the play I have on hand right now – I don't like calling it a sequel to *Song of a Goat* but I'm beginning to think of a three-part play, a trilogy. In this play, for instance, the young wife in *Song of a Goat* who gets into this disaster, is supposed to have a miscarriage of the child she was going to bear for the brother of her husband. I'm thinking of the messenger coming in, for instance, and saying, 'I fear the lady has – the woman has had miscarriage.' What I'm working on now is the story developing from this. I'm taking this line and saying there wasn't any miscarriage after all: she was saved and then the child was born after all, was taken away to another place, to another part of the creeks, then brought up, and he comes back as a grown-up man to another place where he wants to take a wife, and everything goes on pretty fine; but the play is going to open where he is about to take the wife away. Everything has been smooth and perfect and great and then the question crops up: what is this man's background after all? Who knows his family, really? And it turns out he is the son ... you know, he has such and such a background. Now the father-in-law to be takes his turn and says, 'You girl, my daughter, you must not, I mean we've been sort of tainted, plague has come among us!' but the girl refuses and ... well, that's the story in outline. And then I'm thinking of, say, going back and because in *Song of a Goat*, the play as it is today, there is a lot of talk about the ancestors and ancient heroes, Zifa's father, who died of leprosy, of the white taint and then was buried in the evil grove (probably this is one of the places where they say I was influenced by the Greeks), so that ...

NKOSI Yes, this is what one might normally suggest. ...

CLARK ... that the sins of the father are being visited of the son, you see. I'm very tempted now to write the story of the father, maybe when I finish this present sequel play: I don't know how long it is going to take me, but I guess going to Princeton I might have more time on my hands than I have had so far working on a newspaper, you know.

When this discussion was recorded J. P. Clark's *Three Plays* were about to be published by Oxford University Press. The interviewer was Andrew Salkey; it took place as Clark was on his way home from America in January 1964 – the visit which resulted in *America Their America*.

SALKEY   We both begin, J.P., with the language of English, a language in common, a language as it were transplanted from its source in England and used by you in Nigeria and by me in Jamaica. Would you claim to have made the language your own in every possible way or would you say that it is used in Nigeria as half your own and half not?

CLARK   I think I use the language as completely as I can, I don't regard myself as using it half and half with another language maybe providing the full tongue. Personally I find, very often, that a thought you have has been very well expressed already in your mother tongue; you like that manner of expression so much you want to transplant it into English. This is where you have so-called quaintness and the fresh turn of mind and phrase or fresh use of the language. One really doesn't go out of one's way to sound fresh or sound novel – to be quaint or that type of thing. You use the language because it is the best you have to express what you want to say.

SALKEY   Both our countries are now independent, J.P., Nigeria and Jamaica are on their own and with a language which is shared not only by Nigeria and Jamaica but by many other countries. As a matter of fact English binds all of us together and in turn it binds us to England culturally. Think of our particular triangle, Nigeria, England, then you have at the other end Jamaica. Do you see any inherent contradiction in this linguistic link, is there any embarrassment when you sit down to write a poem?

CLARK   No, no I don't find it an embarrassment at all, in fact, I think it is a great richness, a great point of contact and inspiration that so many people in such very distant lands can get to understand one another in one language without the need for an interpreter. I mean as a writer I believe a lot in communication, the greater the number of people I can get to the better for me.

SALKEY   What about the business of poetic diction? Can English express everything a Nigerian poet like yourself may want to express? Aren't there certain Nigerian experiences which might elude English expression, English vocabulary, English syntax and so on? Can English really carry the whole weight of a Nigerian imagination?

CLARK   That is a very controversial point although personally I don't think it's so. I don't know what the Nigerian imagination is really and what the English imagination is, or the Jamaican imagination for that matter. I really don't know it. I suppose you mean writers are born and bred against a certain background, a certain back-drop and therefore they think of this and you find this in their work and all that. If that is what you would call imagination, then I would agree with you. But if you suggest I have thoughts or feelings or insights or intuitive memories or things like that which I find difficult to express in English, as against say expressing in the language my mother and my father speak, I don't think I have that difficulty. I'm not saying that it doesn't exist. It does, but where possible I try to borrow just like the English – those who made the language – I mean they borrow from Latin sources, French sources, wherever possible they still borrow. I think we even have Nigerian words in the language right now, you see: A word like 'palava' or 'palaver' for instance, is typically West African or Nigerian in flavour, despite its European roots.

SALKEY   Our former colonial status has made us – well, willingly or unwillingly – recipients of one or two alien values, J.P., alien standards, aims and aspirations.

CLARK   Like...?

SALKEY   Well take the situation of accepting or, as T. S. Eliot has said, 'appreciating certain realities in a non-real sense', the image of snow for instance in the poem by an English poet whom you and I had to study in the G.C.E. Advanced Level in our secondary schools in Nigeria and Jamaica. How do you feel about this?

CLARK   Spring, summer and all that. It meant nothing to me until I came over this way.

SALKEY   Well, let's take your poem 'Ibadan', one of ten of your own poems included in the Penguin edition of *Modern Poetry from Africa*.* It goes:

> 'Ibadan,
>   running splash of rust
> and gold – flung and scattered
> among seven hills like broken
> china in the sun.'

I like this poem, J.P. Would you say it was your own voice or is it half and half?

CLARK   I don't know whether that's a compliment, Andrew, but do you mean by half and half the image is mine and the language is English – my subject is Nigerian, the largest city in Africa, Ibadan; and then the language I use describing it is English. If that's what you mean by half and half,

* Cf. also *A Reed in the Tide*, p. 12. *Poems* (Mbari), p. 31.

then I would say 'yes'. But this is *my* own single voice coming out, and then I would say there is nothing half and half about this poem.

SALKEY   In the West Indies there are a number of potential writers who will say that, you know, that they wish they would have had the chance to be fed on a diet indigenously their own rather than on a literary diet of Donne and Shakespeare, but the point is we didn't have any diet of our own. What we have had so far is an oral tradition which I think is true of Africa . . .

CLARK   That is very true.

SALKEY   . . . Now we haven't got the written thing yet, we've just begun doing so, you see, the last – what? – the last twelve, fifteen, sixteen years, a number of novels and plays have been published in book form and so on. Therefore I think that it's just a little bit cheating but I wanted to find out what you really thought about this business of an English diet in a Nigerian setting.

CLARK   Right now, there is a big move at home to have on the school syllabus books, plays, poems, novels written by Nigerians. What I meant earlier was that I shared my life sort of and I lived in two worlds, and whenever I went home on holidays, for instance, I still had my family intact, you know. Family didn't just mean mother and father, it meant the whole tree, it meant the whole village – the whole clan – the whole tribe, and things are pretty much intact, you know, as they have always been. And when I went back to school I was sort of, to mix metaphors, sort of swimming around in other streams, you see, and the other one is always there. Now, I suppose this double stream is what you haven't got in the West Indies. All you really have is the English stream and any other thing you did was thought to be barbaric or, you know, a throwback to your African ancestors, the jungle, or something like that.

SALKEY   Yes, I think you are right about us in the West Indies in that regard. The average West Indian, for instance, can out-William Wordsworth, you know, quite easily, or even take the tone of T. S. Eliot and become even more indelibly T. S. Eliot than T. S. Eliot could be.

CLARK   That's unfortunate . . .

SALKEY   Yes, it's frightfully unfortunate and another thing is, we haven't really got anything to reach out to in our past, we tend to live in our present, you know, and it's a state of confusion and so on . . . That aside, we're both – as writers – whether we like it or not, J.P., very much a part of what I would call the main stream of English writing, English contemporary writing and as such we are expected to contribute to it in some way or the other. What would you say is the quality of the contribution from Nigerian writers writing in the English language?

CLARK I'm glad you regard yourself and me as being part of the main stream of English literature.

SALKEY Well, you see, the point is I don't see us in that light but I think that we are seen in that light by a number of responsible critics in this country and elsewhere simply because we use the language in our homes, you see. And we've now turned out novels in the very same language, which are going to be read not only by our own people but by other people, and I do feel that we expect some kind of contribution from – let's say writers like yourself, Cyprian Ekwensi, George Lamming, and so on. And I would imagine that the only contribution that I can think of coming from the Caribbean is one that has to do with the comic imagination. I really feel that West Indians more than any other set of former colonial writers and so on have given a freshness to comedy. People like Samuel Selvon, for instance, they do have a unique way of hitching tragedy and comedy up together and giving you what we call in the dialect 'the bite and the blow' technique; you know – the rat bites into the skin and then blows the spot immediately afterwards. This, I think, is what a number of West Indian writers are doing, a strange quality of comic writing. Well, I think it's the quality of our contributions. That is the thing that really ought to be considered. And I think that the quality coming from the Caribbean is one that is a compound of laughter and tears.

CLARK Each one of us I think we are exploring life as we find it and as we're able to and I suppose the critics would find a lot of things if they're looking for them.

When J. P. Clark was next interviewed by Andrew Salkey, again in London and again during 1964 – but in September this time – *America Their America* had just been published.

SALKEY J.P., I'd like to begin by asking you about the three-way writing life you lead: poetry, playwriting and journalism. Now, other writers find it demanding, to say the least: just how do you cope?

CLARK I allow each impulse to find its own outlet, I don't really find any conflict.

SALKEY I know this question is very nearly impossible to answer with any measure of objectivity, but which of the three forms of writing is the most important to you personally?

CLARK I think journalism reaches the widest public; so too with playwriting, because you may not be literate but you can see the sets, you can hear the dialogue, you can hear the music, you can hear all that and my creation to all that too; but poetry, I think, is my pet medium. I have got a book of poetry coming out very soon with Longmans and another publisher of mine wanted me to wait until next year before they would bring out my selected poems, and I said this is like saying the market for cocoa is bad now so let's wait until it sells before we begin selling palm-oils, you know. I think the two are different things and they should be left to live their own lives. But to return to favourites, to me poetry is the pet medium, and better still if it's used in the theatre.

SALKEY   Equally impossible, I think, J.P., is this next question: which of the three do you think is your most important contribution to West African writing as a whole, and to Nigerian writing in particular?

CLARK   As I said, journalism, of course, carries the news to everybody, every day, and poetry is a very literary art, although I believe my people are a very poetic group, because they often sing and speak incantations, for instance to their Gods. Poetry, I think, is a very popular art among my own people, being spoken in a sung medium, chanted . . . All the same, I think the theatre is a better way, I think the most solid way, if we write in English. There are limitations upon the reach of the written poetic form among a non-literate people as mine are, but in the theatre, even if they don't get the dialogue, they get the actions, as it were; as I said earlier, they appreciate the sets, they appreciate gestures, expressions, movements, they partake of the mood and the dramatic atmosphere, they take part in the music. I think it is the theatre that gets to a non-reading public.

SALKEY   And what do you see as the role, the precise position of the poet in Nigerian society?

CLARK   I think before the poet begins playing any role in Nigerian society, I think he has to recognize himself. He has to find himself really, within this society first, before he knows what role it is really he is playing; because in the search for images, in the search for the most apposite expression you often find you are going back to your people, which means you are going back to your roots, and that means you are going back to the so-called vernacular, you see, and although your writing may be for a very learned audience when you're using English, the mere fact that you are going back to your own people for your images, for your expressions and all that, means that you find yourself in a sort of ambivalent role where you find yourself between the so-called educated and the so-called illiterate. So I think it's a role of reconciliation really, and interpretation.

SALKEY   Is this also true about the playwright, just what is his position?

CLARK   I think the playwright functions very much like the poet; as I said poetry in its most effective form should be in theatre. . . . I think the roles are more or less alike; or rather, very much alike.

SALKEY   And the journalist? I'm thinking exclusively of the quality journalist – what's his contribution like, what ought it to be?

CLARK   Well in Nigeria, for instance, the journalistic profession, I'm sorry to say, has always been an unfortunate one; it's only in recent years that it's won some respect for itself, but as a profession to begin with, it never had any chance beside the legal profession or the medical profession or any of the other 'learned' professions. People always felt in Nigeria that journalism was something you went to when you'd failed in all the others: you couldn't get into a university, you couldn't get into some professional, respectable group, so you drifted into journalism, and I'm afraid that even those within – the greatest practitioners of – journalism in Nigeria today sort of lend credit and creditability to this because it was my feeling, during the one or two years I spent on newspapers in Nigeria, that when you had gone through a university, or you had written poetry or plays or things like that, you were looked on as a sort of interloper when you came into a newspaper office. I think it is a very responsible profession, it should be, and I wouldn't say it is the least of the three interests I have.

SALKEY   I'd like now to come to your most recent book, *America Their America*. For me it's the first of it's kind from any living negro author, J.P. In a way it's polemical journalism, it's quality reporting, it's also a distinguished travel book. What made you write it?

CLARK   It was just the experience of America: I felt I had to get it out of my system, either by way of reporting – and eventually I did, I found an outlet by way of this straight reporting – or by way of verse, or by way of commentary, but I just had to get that experience out of my system.

SALKEY   Do you know *America Their America* might well become a trend-setter for certain African writers who might see in its style and in its content, a very definite way of addressing themselves to non-Africans. Do you think I'm right about this? In other words, is *America Their America* going to mean that much to West African writers that they would want to follow through in its shape and in its pattern?

CLARK   Well, I hope it becomes seminal in the way you mean, but *America Their America* was written for Americans, for Europeans, for Africans, for everybody. America is a big mother for everybody, except if you are on the left-hand side of the walls you know, but she is a big Auntie for everybody, you know, and if a sort of wastrel fellow like me goes to America and has been fêted all over the place and yet returns home to spew out this type of thing, I think, I can only hope that it will make other people look around and see that the drink doesn't go to their heads, and the fine dinner set and all the fine food. If despite the fêting they do keep their heads, they can later say what they actually saw and how they saw it, and how they actually felt over there. If it does that then for the white man, for the black man, for the blue man, for the yellow or red man, then I think it has done its job, you know.

SALKEY One last question, J.P. So far, where would you say that the non-fiction, the poetry, the plays, the novels and the better forms of journalism in Africa are actually headed, what's the new direction?

CLARK I wonder, I really wonder, simply because in West Africa I think we are very . . . it's really Nigeria – I shouldn't say in West Africa as a whole; except in Sierra Leone, perhaps in Gambia, I think in Ghana things are more organized, as you know, but I think in Nigeria writers are more or less on their own, there's a lonely search. I think it should be so, so that you make your discovery or you get lost at your own risk. I don't know in what direction it's moving. I don't think there's any one direction it's moving to. I think it's an individual search, experimenting. I think writing is experimenting, you know. We'll have to wait and see.

Cyprian Ekwensi
BORN 1921

▼▼▼▼▼▼▼▼▼▼▼▼▼▼▼▼▼▼▼▼▼▼▼▼▼▼▼▼

This interview with Lewis Nkosi was made when Cyprian Ekwensi was Director of the Information Services of Nigeria. It was recorded in August 1962 in Lagos.

At that time Ekwensi had published the following books: *When Love Whispers* (1947), *The Leopard's Claw* (1947), *Okolo the Wrestler* (Nelson 1947), *For a Roll of Parchment* (1951), *Beware of the Bight of Benin* (1951), *The Passport of Mallam Ilia* (C.U.P. 1960), *The Drummer Boy* (C.U.P. 1960).

The following are mentioned in this interview: *People of the City* (Dakers, London 1954 and Heinemann 1962), *Jagua Nana* (Hutchinson 1961), *Burning Grass* (Heinemann 1962) which was about to be published: *Beautiful Feathers* (Hutchinson 1963 and Heinemann 1970), *Yaba Roundabout Murder* (Tortoise Series Book, Lagos 1962) *Iska* (Hutchinson 1966) and *Lokotown and other stories* (Heinemann 1966).

NKOSI Mr Ekwensi, I understand that your latest novel, *Jagua Nana*, is about to be filmed by an Italian company. As it is, you are already a popular novelist, and perhaps most readers of your books would like to find out a bit about you, just how you work and what kind of attitude you have to literature as a whole. So, to begin, about what time did you really begin to write?

EKWENSI I think I began to write as early as twenty-one years ago, actually. This was in the Higher College – it was then called the Higher College, sort of post-secondary school; there wasn't any university in Nigeria at that time, you see, and I wrote mainly for a school magazine called *The Viking*. But later on I went into the Forestry Department of the Federal Government, and in the days in the forest I was able to reminisce and write. That was when I really began to write for publishing.

NKOSI Which is your first book?

EKWENSI Well, my first book is something printed in Nigeria called *When Love Whispers*, it's a novelette really, it's a little love story of a girl who loves a boy who goes to England hoping she will marry him, and then when he returns she is already married.

NKOSI   Since that book, how many books have you written?

EKWENSI   Well, I think I've written altogether about eighteen; I've published twelve – about twelve.

NKOSI   And is *Jagua Nana* the most successful?

EKWENSI   *Jagua* is the most successful of the lot.

NKOSI   For which of these works have you got the highest regard ... Artistically?

EKWENSI   Well, artistically, I think I have the highest regard for my short stories, not necessarily for that novel, the short stories I wrote about a rustic people, the Fulani, among whom I lived for about three weeks. Sentimentally speaking, the best liked of my works is *People of the City* which is a little thing I turned out based on a number of short stories I wrote for Radio Nigeria.

NKOSI   It was interesting in *People of the City* that you captured so well the Lagos atmosphere, the atmosphere of the city, so that one was able to know just what kind of city is in Africa. I just wonder why you think there isn't enough social criticism in the books written about the urban situation in Nigeria, say about slums. One of the criticisms I've heard about *Jagua Nana*, for instance, is that there is no moral censure; now do you agree with this criticism or not?

EKWENSI   Well, you see, we are in an era now when we want to see only what might be described as the prestige side of our lives but the true artist doesn't look for the prestige side. He looks for life in its sordidness or life at its most glorious: true life still has its own particular fascination for the writer. Well then, if you want to do a prestige novel, get a government agency, pay him, and there he goes: he closes his eyes to everything else and gives you what would be very stilted, nobody would like to read it, it would cost a lot of money and it would be untrue. But if you want real life you must go down to the people and that is what I always do in my novels. A writer writes fiction but fiction is based on fact, and even though you may have a fictitious character he may be a composite of many different characters and perhaps to a certain extent recognizable as one, or many people may recognize certain qualities in that individual. This goes to show that it's fact, and the mere fact that my readers feel uncomfortable means they think they're reading the sort of truth which they think should not be told, and I do not agree with that.

NKOSI   Tell me, sir, just what kind of audience have you got in mind when you write: do you write for an overseas audience or do you write for the Nigerian one?

EKWENSI Well, I write for both, I am a writer. I think I am a writer who regards himself as a writer for the masses.

I don't think of myself as a literary stylist: if my style comes, that is just incidental, but I am more interested in getting at the heart of the truth which the man in the street can recognize than in just spinning words. I believe that if you have the real guts of it in your work it will come out, and it will be recognizable, it will have a smell to it which any reader, even though he hasn't been there, will identify, as opposed to mere beautiful words which you can write from afar.

NKOSI Yes. Which one of these books gave you the most trouble in doing and which one did you find easier?

EKWENSI I found *Jagua* – actually the conception of *Jagua* took place two years before it was published, the actual writing I did in twelve days. *People of the City* I wrote in ten days. You wanted to know how I work: you see, I work intensively; I believe in getting it all done; I believe in digesting my material: I'm not one of those writers who don't know where they're going when they start. When I start a novel I know what is going to happen to every character, although it doesn't always turn out altogether like that: some of the surprises are very pleasant, you find a minor character who didn't even appear on your synopsis suddenly beginning to grow big and to overshadow others – well that sort of thing is unpredictable but I generally and very roughly have an idea of where I am going and as a result of that I am able to keep going from day to day. I do not have the author's tantrums of biting the end of the pencil for days waiting for inspiration. I just go on writing till I get to the end, then I go over it and polish.

Talking about actual mechanical writing, I cannot write fast enough to keep pace with my thoughts with a pen or pencil, I write straight on the typewriter.

NKOSI If we might next get to this question, who amongst the writers of modern literature or classical literature has influenced you most? Who is your favourite writer?

EKWENSI Well, I should say a multitude. As regards working methods there are two people who have influenced me most – one is Simenon, who writes a novel in ten days, and the other is Edgar Wallace who used to write a novel in two days.

With regard to style, all of us owe something to Hemingway, I owe something to Steinbeck, Maupassant, Flaubert – all these are my favourite writers. But whenever I want to write and whenever I want to experience a certain humility I go back to Chekov and read him; sometimes I read *Anna Karenina*, I just read a part of *Anna Karenina*, either the brother who was very consumptive or Anna herself at the railway station going to be crushed by a train, and it's incredible the effect it has – it's a very deep sort of worship as far as I'm concerned.

NKOSI   There is at the moment in Nigeria at Ibadan the Mbari Writers' and Artists' Club and around this club is centred a school of young writers in Nigeria today. I wonder whether are you in contact with most of these people or do you lead an isolated life?

EKWENSI   No, I don't lead an isolated life. I have recently formed a Society of Nigerian Authors and had the honour to be made President, because I felt that Nigeria, being an independent country, must have a contact body: sometimes writers come here and they want to know what the writers are doing here, they should go to a body like the Society of Nigerian Authors.

Mbari is sponsored by the Congress for African Freedom; I am in touch with them, I know the young writers, I have recently judged a short story competition in which most of the young writers participated and I receive, like every writer whose name has appeared before the world, I receive unsolicited manuscripts, authors coming to me for help. The other day someone wanted me to pay his fare back home!

NKOSI   Now just a bit about *Jagua Nana*, what latest arrangements are there for the final filming of the work?

EKWENSI   The work is to be filmed in the dry season, that is end of October, beginning of November, or roundabout the middle of November. And the company is called Delphia, it's a new company, but all the members are old and famous film-makers. The producer is going to be Alberto Latuada who's well-known internationally. And Italy, as you know, is an up-and-coming centre for film-making, almost stealing the Oscar from Hollywood.

NKOSI   And what tribe do you belong to in Nigeria?

EKWENSI   Well, I come from Eastern Nigeria, I am an Ibo.

At the time of the next interview (with Dennis Duerden, in London, during November 1964) Ekwensi had just been to a conference organized by the American Society for African Culture at Cleveland, Ohio, where Ekwensi had read a paper on the novel in Africa.

DUERDEN   Can you tell us something about your paper and what sort of questions were asked about it?

EKWENSI   In my paper – 'Theme in the African novel' – I tried to explore the themes usually pursued by African writers and I broke the subject down into the following parts: the theme in the West African novel deals either with the multi-racial society or with change in what I might call rural society – change in village life owing to the intrusion of perhaps Western civilization or what have you; and there is also the 'man of two worlds' theme. Whereas 'theme' in the South African novel is usually a protest, a cry against apartheid and 'theme' in the Negro American novel is the blues theme – the theme of the negro striving for equal rights with white people. The aim of this paper was to show that a novel does not necessarily qualify as an African novel because it deals with say a ritual and other things like that. A novel qualifies as an African novel if it puts forward African psychology and this is inherent in the novel whether it is set in Independence Square in Dakar or in a village in Eastern Nigeria.

DUERDEN   That is an interesting definition of the African novel and one which I haven't heard before. A number of people have struggled very hard to try to say what makes African literature 'African' and I think this sounds as if it might be a most interesting approach. There is one question I would like to ask you about your own novels and that is that in portraying this African psychology you are often accused of portraying features of African life which modern African governments don't want to be circulated widely outside Africa. Do you find any conflict between your work as a Director of Information who has to interpret the wishes of government and as a novelist? I was thinking in particular of your book *Jagua Nana* which I suppose is the most famous.

EKWENSI   Well, the duty of a novelist and the duty of a playwright, the duty of any fiction writer is to seek truth. He has to go down to truth; truth can be seen in many facets. I don't know if you remember the Japanese film 'Rashomon', in which a woman tells a story that she was raped in the middle of a forest. Now this is the simple story of 'Rashomon' and then we begin to see this incident through various eyes – the man himself, who is a soldier who is accused of this – the woman herself and so on. It is the duty of the novelist like a surgeon to keep dissecting until he gets to this cancer, to the truth, to where truth is embedded, and the novelist does not attempt to portray a government or a nation, the novelist goes into individual souls and hearts. This is why, as I said earlier on, Wole Soyinka's play *The Trials of Brother Jero*, was performed by American negroes and it went down as well as if it had been written for them because that novel contains the fundamental truth of the hypocritical priest who on the one hand is telling you about God and on the other hand will not pay his debts and is seducing his congregation and so on. Now in that play, for instance, there is no attempt to portray Nigeria as such, he is portraying the type of individual who behaves like that and this is what I try to do in my novels. It does not matter whether I am portraying a band leader or a bad woman with a good heart or whatever it is, these people are not peculiar to Nigeria – they exist everywhere – and I think it is the wrong approach to begin to think of a novel in terms of a country unless of course it happens to be a propaganda novel, then that is a different thing. When Dickens was writing his novels about the slum areas of London he wasn't trying to portray London as such, he was trying to portray these voracious, money-grabbing school proprietors who would always want to get just the money and nothing else, they have nothing else to offer for that.

Now, there are money-grabbing school proprietors today in any part of the world. This is why governments have legislated and have to examine every school according to certain standards. A school has to be approved and all that kind of thing, you see. So I think it is a wrong approach for anyone to imagine a Director of Information Services whose duty on the one side is to deal with facts and who happens to be a fiction writer seeking truth, seeking out the imperfection of man – which is a universal thing – to be at odds with himself. There is no conflict at all as far as I am concerned and the duties are not contradictory.

DUERDEN Do you see your novels as some kind of social commentary, I mean, saying something about the state of present-day Nigeria or present-day Lagos?

EKWENSI Yes, my novels are social commentary incidentally. I don't set out to make my novels social commentary. If any social commentary emerges then this is something which the reader is left to get out of it for himself. I am primarily a story-teller. I am interested in the story – this is what interests me. In *Beautiful Feathers* I tell a story of a man who is trying to unite the whole of Africa, whereas at home he has no control over his wife; his home life from which the unity should begin is uneven; he is not a leader in his own home. This is a very interesting theme. And there is in *Jagua Nana* – I am also dealing with an individual – a bad woman: it is just a story of a woman who thinks her future is coming to an end and she invests in a young man who gets educated and therefore carries her for the rest of her life.

DUERDEN Well, then, can I put the question another way? You seem to have a tremendous amount of compassion for the characters in your novels in a somewhat Dickensian way. I mean, you were talking about Dickens and the parallel seems true – from reading your novels one feels that you sort of feel for these people and the predicament they are in. Do you as a writer feel that you are expressing your compassion for these people, for their predicament?

EKWENSI Well, there again I think that comes out from the reading. I never consciously do that but as you know me, Dennis, you know that I love Nigeria and I know it backwards having been born in the North, raised in the West, and of Eastern origin, and every year I go round Nigeria two or three times by car, by road, so I know my country and I love it.

I think every writer basically loves nature and this comes out in the novel, any false note you can immediately detect. Perhaps you've detected this love but it is not meant as a primary aim, as I say, I am primarily interested in the story of the individual.

DUERDEN Do you find that your feelings about your characters are pessimistic ones, I mean do you feel that they are in a position from which they find it difficult to escape?

EKWENSI Yes, yes, they are pessimistic ones because I look at life with the boy scout's eye of 'be prepared' ... for the worst you see! And although they are pessimistic they are not all pessimistic: there are happy ones, and I feel a good deal of compassion for the characters.

DUERDEN Well, Cyprian, I believe you have finished another novel?

EKWENSI Oh no, no this is putting words into my mouth, I am working on another novel.

DUERDEN Can you say something about what this one will be?

EKWENSI Well, it is a very simple novel, it is the story of a girl. This is a girl – you'll accuse me of being pessimistic again – this is a girl whose life ends very tragically when she is very young and with a very bright future and it is quite contrary to the expectations of the people who love her, and so the circumstances in which she just loses her life awaken a very great deal of reaction in the hearts of people who are, in one way or the other, connected with her. This is the story and I have decided to call it *Iska*: you speak Hausa, so you know that Iska is Wind. The wind blows, you don't see it, it has passed even before you know it has blown, so this girl's life just blows like that – like wind.

Mazisi Kunene
BORN 1930

▼▼▼▼▼▼▼▼▼▼▼▼▼▼▼▼▼▼▼▼▼▼▼▼▼▼▼▼▼

At the time of the first interview with Lewis Nkosi in May 1964, Mazisi Kunene was in London as the representative in the United Kingdom and in Europe of the African National Congress of South Africa. He had originally come to Britain to do research in comparative literature and especially to complete a doctoral thesis on Zulu literature. His own voluminous poetic output was still largely unavailable in English, scattered poems were then to be found in magazines, and the only collection in a book was four poems in Gerald Moore and Ulli Beier's *Modern Poetry from Africa* (Penguin).
Critical articles by Kunene were similarly scattered. Since then more have appeared, particularly in *The New African, Sechaba* and *Afro-Asian Writings*.
In 1969, Kunene contributed an introduction to a new translation of Aimé Cesaire's *Return To My Native Land* (Penguin) and in 1970, he published *Zulu Poems* (André Deutsch).

NKOSI Raymond, you are a poet who has written poetry in Zulu as well as in English. Do you feel that an African poet has anything to learn from Shakespeare?

KUNENE Well, I certainly think so, as any poet benefits from the works of other writers, other poets in any other country.

NKOSI Is there something special that an African poet might learn from Shakespeare? Or, narrowing it down that a South African poet might learn . . .

KUNENE Oh, I think a poet can learn quite a lot from Shakespeare precisely because of his objective analysis of society, of individuals in society, and also from his use of language as a vehicle of communication in expressing what is contained in the character or depicting the character involved.

NKOSI Yes, now though you talk about his objective depiction of character, many people have quarrelled with Shakespeare's depiction of the negro. How do you feel about that particular area of Shakespeare's artistic function?

KUNENE Well, Shakespeare depicted the negro ... But in fact, I think the premise of their quarrel and of your question is wrong in the sense that one thinks of Shakespeare as depicting negro character. I think at the time when Shakespeare wrote there wasn't the same amount of racial tension as exists today. He was merely depicting character. It might be true that the negro had special appeal to Europe because he was not then common in Europe, but I don't think Shakespeare was in fact thinking of the racial qualities. I think he depicted a situation which might arise if the two people of different cultural origins perhaps came together. In *Othello*, for instance, I think he is concerned more with the possible conflict between the two people, not as racial entities but as two individuals coming from different cultures.

NKOSI You have studied Zulu poetry, especially what you call the classical period of Zulu poetry. Can you tell me whether you find any similarities in the development of Zulu poetry at this time and Shakespeare's own development or what he contributed to the English language during the Elizabethan period of English literature?

KUNENE Well, yes and no; I think yes, because the Elizabethan period contained in it the same characteristics of nationalism. Then there was also a certain amount, perhaps a large amount of violence; but in South Africa I think the nationalism expressed has not really succeeded in finding concrete forms of expression so that there is in fact a struggle towards an objective depiction of your own situation. And now the individuals in South Africa are fully involved in the present-day, internal situation, whereas in the Elizabethan period it was a nationalism expressing itself outwardly if you like.

NKOSI Yes, and of course people remark on Shakespeare's affection for large gestures, for vivid imagery and I know that certain Africans in South Africa would sometimes borrow from Shakespeare's plays, borrow expressions, because they felt that these expressions came naturally to them, so they would declaim in the streets because they loved this language of gesture. Is there anything in the urban life of South Africa that is equivalent to the urban life of Elizabethan England?

KUNENE I think it's mainly what one would call the dramatic tension that exists in the situation. In England you found exactly the same thing, the spectacle, and the love of swords, fighting and so on. In urban life today in South Africa you get exactly about the same thing. Not the idealization of violence as such (I don't say Shakespeare did idealize violence, as such), but a writer who writes truthfully, depicts a situation as he sees it. He must depict the spectacle that exists, the dramatic tension that exists in the country – in the South Africa of today – in the same way that Shakespeare did. So, I think when you talk of the love of the African to use the Shakespearian texture of language, it's mainly because I think Shakespeare is so objective in his approach or, subjective-objective (if there could be something like that) in his approach, that there is a possibility of understanding his plays on two planes: from the angle of the actual story, what is told, the particular spectacle, and this could often have been anywhere in Africa: and then also on another level, the symbolic level in which he depicted a human situation not as a periodic situation, only of that particular period, but what would happen to human life under such circumstances. Well, I think you get this also in African literature, where you get the story, which can be enjoyed as a story by itself. At the same time if you are intelligent enough you are able to understand the symbolic meaning contained in the story, which is of course, higher than the sort of apparent story level.

NKOSI According to the critic George Steiner, tragedy has died and one of the reasons why people feel that tragedy is no longer possible in modern life, is that instead of having one hero suffering for the whole society now we have what one might call collective suffering or collective heroism and this is mainly because of the advent of democracy. Do you think that in Africa we have reached the same stage?

KUNENE Well, I don't like to think in these stages, of us in Africa reaching a stage. I think this is mainly in Europe. Perhaps Europe suffers from a collective neurosis so that everybody suffers from a common disease and so there are certain diseases that are tabulated and one expects that in the depiction of character it should be all the other people expressed or depicted in terms of the psychological approach. Whereas in Africa I think it's a different situation. The hero is very much there and the values associated with the social individual, the contribution of the individual to society is still very, very much a high ideal, whereas in Europe, there is an excess of individualism, a 'self'-contained type of approach to the problems of society, so that as such the artist himself sees human society in Europe chiefly in terms of what he reads from Freud, and in terms of general abstractions, rather than in terms of individual action in relation to society or to neighbour or to the next person.

The next interview with Kunene was recorded in October 1966, in London, Alex la Guma interviewing. At that time Kunene was the African National Congress (S.A.) representative in the United Kingdom and Europe and was running their London office.

LA GUMA Raymond, how do you manage to work, not on one, but on two major works, and still continue to conduct political activity?

KUNENE Well, I think the essence of writing is really the combination between the two: I think in the tradition generally in Africa there has never been a period in which there was an absolute separation between, here, the act of writing or creating artistically, and, there, everyday life; and I think one is able to do this because the two are in fact intertwined, the spirit of political change and activity is inevitably transposed on to the works that one creates.

LA GUMA Now at the moment you are writing two epic poems: will you tell us about them.

KUNENE Well, one epic deals with the creation, the origin of life, the concept of the origin of life held by an indigenous African community. And since this is a discussion, basically, about a philosophy of life (which I think is what any religion is), the social expression of the philosophy of life of a particular community; the epic then deals with this philosophy, the beliefs in the organization of society, the beliefs in the ultimate destinies of man, and the belief in the actual history of the community itself.

And the second epic is concerned with the history of the rise and fall of the Zulu empire,

LA GUMA With regard to your first epic, I presume that your interpretation of these concepts of the origin of life and the universe will of necessity also be an exploration of the underlying philosophy which binds African society.

KUNENE Certainly. The point of the epic is really to show how the social organization in Africa is expressed in the philosophy that binds this society together. And indeed, I think in the nature of African society there is a sense of continuity, from the past, and the present, and the future, and this sense of continuity is in fact the basic philosophy in African life. As you know, African life is organized in communal form, and the emphasis is always in the respect of the individual belonging to the community itself and on services that the individual performs in relation to the community, and therefore the emphases are on the social obligations of the individual to the community. Hence, I think, the emphasis on heroism as the highest mode of social expression, as opposed, I believe, to the sense of justice, which I think is relevant in societies which are fragmented and therefore represent in essence a compromise between the conflicting interests.

LA GUMA   Tell me, to what sort of extent does this philosophy differ from philosophy evolved in Europe?

KUNENE   Well, I think it's different because the European society for a long time has been organized in individualistic terms; in Africa, as I said, it's organized in communal forms. As a result in Europe, I think, the emphasis has always been on an individual, and therefore the emphasis is always on the expressions and the exchange of conversation between individuals in art and drama, in every aspect. Whereas in Africa the emphasis is always on the symbol, the symbol which in essence is the representation of the attitude of the community, and in fact, it is the easiest access to a communal expression, for it contains communal meaning.

LA GUMA   And now, briefly, returning to your second epic poem. Can you tell us briefly what this deals with?

KUNENE   The history of the rise and fall of the Zulu empire, but here I'm not concerned with the Zulu empire as such, I'm concerned with it as a historical experience of a particular sector of mankind, and therefore I am not concerned with the sloganizing of the Zulu empire, nor am I concerned with the glorification of the Zulu empire, but with depicting it as part of an experience of a particular community. I think here you'll see the genius of the particular orientation of the Shaka period, of Shaka who I think was a great political and military genius, and I hope to show all these aspects and experience of man under these circumstances.

LA GUMA   Raymond, the history of the African people has been minimized in text books, particularly in South Africa. Will you in your epic attempt to place African history in its proper perspective?

KUNENE   I think this is absolutely essential. Not because of any chauvinistic attitude, but it is essential, as you point out, because of the minimization of African history and so on, and I think it's essential in this sense: that in any situation where there is a need for or the demand for nation building, it is necessary to create, in the artistic and perhaps in the political world, a national ego. And I think this national ego must in its essence express the general experience of mankind, and that general experience I think in turn, must emphasize the oneness and the unity of man. And I think that the important thing in doing this is that you in fact release the energies of the particular community, and it's able to reflect and create perspectives for its development, and its expression in general, realizing its context in the whole history of mankind.

Alex la Guma
BORN 1925

▼▼▼▼▼▼▼▼▼▼▼▼▼▼▼▼▼▼▼▼▼▼▼▼▼▼▼▼

This interview with Robert Serumaga was recorded in London in October 1966.
At that time Alex la Guma had published: *A Walk in the Night* (Mbari 1962. It was later reissued with some of his stories by Heinemann) and *And a Three-fold Cord* (Seven Seas 1964).
More of his stories had appeared in anthologies and in magazines such as *Black Orpheus* and *The New African*. He was one of four contributors to *Quartet* edited by Richard Rive (Heinemann 1963).
A novel, *The Stone Country* (Seven Seas) was to be published in 1967, and another novel, *In the Fog of the Seasons' End* (Heinemann) in 1972.

SERUMAGA   Alex la Guma, would you tell me where you spent your early life and how it was in South Africa?

LA GUMA   Well, I was born in Cape Town in the area known as District Six. That is the predominantly poor area, inhabited by people of the working class of the Cape Coloured community – that is the designation given by the policies of ethnic partition and by the government of South Africa. It was the early part of my life there that inspired me to write, first a few short stories, and finally a novel, *A Walk in the Night*, which was based on some of my experiences and some of the experiences of friends and other people whom I met during those years.

SERUMAGA   This book, *A Walk in the Night*, is concerned with the situation in South Africa as it affects the individual and what goes on, not only in the physical sense, but what goes on in the mind. You do at the same time write about characters like the policemen from the Afrikaner community. How difficult do you find it to project yourself into the character of an Afrikaner police officer with whom you haven't lived and to make him, as you do, really an individual in himself.

LA GUMA   Well, I think the advantage is that the Cape Coloured community is composed of people descended from an old mixture of the Afrikaner people and the early aborigines. The background of the Coloured people themselves is to a large extent Afrikaans – and English – so I didn't find much difficulty from that point of view, and I might add that I don't think that in background the Afrikaner people – the White people in general – are very different from the Coloured community, so that there wasn't much difficulty in creating that character.

SERUMAGA It has been said that many of the African writers from South Africa (I use the term 'African' to include the Coloured community) are preoccupied with the colour problem. And that many of them do not create individuals, but figures within a situation: they are more interested in the situation than in the individual. Would you think this true of many South African writers?

LA GUMA Well, it's true and I think that it's inevitable – having to live in a society based upon racial discrimination, one where people are set virtually into compartments. Black and White and Coloured, Indian. Whatever opinion they have to express inevitably becomes involved with the impact of this situation, this colour situation, on them. The difficulty, of course, is to try to project oneself across the colour line and I think that is where most writers have failed or have met with extreme difficulty. The problem is living in one set compartment and knowing only of your own life and then trying to project yourself into the life or the environment of another part, of another party.

SERUMAGA You have said that in fact you have lived many of the things that appear in your novel, *A Walk in the Night*, and in the short stories. Now if we take a character like Michael Adonis, who is the main character in your novel, what experiences of his have you lived, and how much is he you?

LA GUMA I've forgotten what my own book is about. Still, Michael Adonis I tried to make a typical Coloured person. During the years I lived in District Six I played with and met characters like him – young men who, because of their situation in life and because of the lack of opportunity and because of their colour have been prevented from achieving anything progressive and from achieving any ambitions – have been forced into Michael's situation. So that what Adonis experienced in the book, I haven't personally experienced as an individual: I have seen it going on around me. That made it easy for me to write and to create such a character.

SERUMAGA The South African situaton is clearly one that is very oppressive. Now, how does this affect a creative writer? What I am saying is here you have a lot of things that one could write about: the human situation itself. But since the writer himself is involved in this, he might find himself unable to create a kind of aesthetic distance, the frame within which his work is created. Now you as a writer: does this oppression inspire you or does it inhibit you or would you write better if you were completely out of the situation?

LA GUMA Well, as far as the inspiration goes, I think what I found is that it has inspired me to expose the situation with a view of changing people's ideas about what is happening in South Africa – or their acceptance of ideas, so that they can move forward to take down the barriers which exist between different peoples. As I said earlier, the problem is the compartments into which people are divided that imbue them with set ideas, set opinions about their positions – and the difficulty is getting people to rid themselves of the situation. As a writer, I try to achieve a universality of opinion and ideas because I believe that writers are not confined to one set of particular compartments. The writer tries to spread out, extend his views, extend his opinions and get opinions from other sources so that he doesn't become confined to his little ivory tower! The danger in South Africa is that writers can become confined, compartmentalized, and many writers have taken the easy way out, of writing only of what they know and not attempting to go beyond that. But even if one has to write within a milieu, a particular environment, or portray a particular environment, I believe that universal ideas can still be expressed within that milieu, within that environment so that your writing does not become confined. Although your stage may be set in a particular environment, your ideas and your writing are not confined.

SERUMAGA Well, I think it might be fair to say that a great majority of the South African writers at the moment have not succeeded to do this particular thing that you are describing now. It has been suggested by some critics of African literature that perhaps the best thing would be to suspend literature altogether in South Africa until the situation was solved, since so many writers cannot go above it and become universal enough. What is your comment about this?

LA GUMA Well, I don't agree with that. I believe that there has been a lot said about South Africa but very little said about what the non-white people in particular are really experiencing. Writers have tried to describe the situation in South Africa in general but very little has been said about the different 'national' groups and the people who live in South Africa. For instance I don't think a great deal has been said about the Coloured community or about the Indian community and I think that even within a framework of racial separateness there is a task which writers have to perform. That is at least letting the world know what is happening – even within their compartments.

Ezekiel Mphahlele
BORN 1919

▼▼▼▼▼▼▼▼▼▼▼▼▼▼▼▼▼▼▼▼▼▼▼▼▼▼▼

This interview was made by Dennis Duerden in June 1963 at the Conference on African Literature in University Curricula at Fourah Bay College, Freetown, Sierra Leone.

At that time Mphahlele had published critical articles, short stories and a few poems in a great number of journals, newspapers and magazines. *Man Must Live and other stories* had been published in Cape Town (The African Bookman 1947).

Other books were: *The African Image* (Faber 1962), *The Living and Dead and other stories* (Black Orpheus 1961) and *Down Second Avenue* (Faber 1959). At about this time there appeared a pamphlet by Mphahlele on the craft of writing.

He later edited *Modern African Stories* (Faber 1964) with Ellis Ayitey Komey and *African Writing Today* (Penguin 1967).

A second collection of his own short stories was to be published as *In Corner B* (EAPH, Nairobi 1967) and a prize-winning novel, *The Wanderers* has been published by Macmillan in New York and London (1971).

DUERDEN   Zeke, would you begin by telling me what the purpose of this conference is?

MPHAHLELE   The purpose of this conference is to talk about African literature with the aim of persuading universities to integrate the teaching of African writing in their normal syllabuses. We had a conference last week in Dakar – a counterpart of this one – on French literature: French African writing is to be introduced in university teaching programmes, and we are dealing here with English African writing. There has been a number of papers read so far on the importance of, and the place of, literature in universities, also the place of African literature in the syllabuses of the future, the practical problems involved. The content of teaching has also been discussed and then there's going to be a panel of writers to answer questions from the conference on their writings.

DUERDEN   Can you tell me what you think the practical results of the conference will be?

MPHAHLELE   According to the reports published on these two conferences, the one in Dakar and this one, the report will be both in French and in English and will reflect all the discussions that have been held in the two places. These reports will be sent out to universities as a practical guide because they intend for instance tomorrow to crystallize our discussions into practical recommendations and this will go into the report, and when universities read this, we hope they will see the way clear to introducing African writing in the university syllabuses.

DUERDEN   What do you think has come out of the conference with particular regard to the teaching of African literature in universities?

MPHAHLELE   We want to liberalize the teaching of literature in universities. We have discovered that a number of the universities in this continent teach literature according to the traditions of British universities, as many of these universities were attached to British universities by special relationships; now we hope that the introduction of African writing into university teaching will help liberalize this. We try now to get rid of all the old systems of teaching and of the old syllabuses, replete with writers who were completely incomprehensible to Africans, and packed with English writing into which the African students cannot readily project themselves. Well, now, African literature, being produced out of the African experience which the African students share, will certainly help liberalize the literature programme of the university. We want not only to teach African writing; of course, we are going to teach, we want to teach literature as literature, African literature being part of it, but whatever else is being taught, we hope that it will be something that the African student and the African teacher can identify himself with.

DUERDEN   Do you think that some new idea of the role of the departments of English literature in African universities has emerged from this conference?

MPHAHLELE   I think it has emerged, there is no doubt about it. There are quite a few lecturers of English in this continent who have not been emancipated yet, who are not convinced yet of the importance of African writing in university teaching and the trend of discussion shows this, but we are hoping that these will be got round to the idea and it will also – I think the idea itself will help bring in a completely new focus on the teaching of literature.

DUERDEN   There seems to have been some kind of re-examination on the parts of the teachers of English literature who are here. I heard one teacher say that he thought that the purpose of teaching English literature was to provide students with a body of one country's literature so that they could see the integrity of a literature. What would you say about this comment?

MPHAHLELE   I shouldn't say that really: I should say to gain the value of what you do in literature, you want to be exposed to the various literatures of the world, good literature and meaningful literature – you don't want to build a ghetto around the literature, around literature in such a way that – as somebody suggested – you'll create a kind of literary Bantustan. You want to cover a broad plain, a broad landscape of literature that will be English, African, Australian, American, Canadian, or European literature itself in translation. This is the kind of thing that we are thinking of, rather than balkanizing literature.

DUERDEN   Another comment I've heard was that literature in the old university curriculum was somehow out of touch with life, that it had to be brought into touch with people's lives around them and that this was a good reason for introducing African literature into the university curriculum. But it seems to me that it is impossible to introduce African literature all at once, even though most of the teachers here seem to be prepared to accept modifications to their curriculum. If one is going to remodel the curriculum on the basis of African life and have a literature which is grounded in African life, is there enough African literature to start doing this?

MPHAHLELE   You are quite right. Yes, it has to be done by bits and pieces as African writing is being produced, but, even then, right from the beginning I would like to see a very drastic change in the university syllabuses and bring them closer in touch with the student experience. There is at any rate, good literature to begin with; if not for a full curriculum, certainly enough to start in the first year already. I don't think we should try to pedal softly at all, we need to be completely drastic. The literature itself that was being taught before, and that's being taught even in British universities at the moment, is appallingly out of touch with reality. A number of things which the students read are quite agonizing and the student gets very little out of it and loses the idea of literature as something that can be enjoyed. Literature can be a discipline but it mustn't be such a discipline that it has to be out of touch with life, and I think there is already a body of African writing which can be taught. Also we need to translate oral literature into English and make it available to a universal audience and this can form part of the English syllabus as something to begin with, something that will introduce the student into poetry, into the enjoyment of the poetry which after all also has its roots in African speech – in African literature.

DUERDEN   There are lots of suggestions from some of the teachers here that you should only choose good works of African literature. It was all right to accept African literature into the curriculum provided they passed some kind of standard or other. Would you say that it is necessary only to have some kind of good African writing, or African writing which is in some way predictably great?

MPHAHLELE I think ideally yes we should introduce literature that is predictably great, not only literature that is good, African writing that is good, especially now that there is a good deal that is promising it is just as well that the student should know what is a good work and what is a work that merely has promise. It also helps them in sharpening their critical faculties or in bringing forth their critical equipment, this learning of literature produced by their own people. I wouldn't say that only very good literature should be brought in but also African writing which is meaningful and has promise. It ought to be brought in.

DUERDEN Let me ask you one final question. Do you think that there is enough good African literature to compose such a university syllabus at the moment or is the discussion in this conference mainly aimed at producing a situation in which there will be in future?

MPHAHLELE I think your latter suggestion is the truer one. There isn't enough, we are not writing fast enough, and there are only few African writers in the field. I should imagine that we should really be concerned in bringing in what does exist that is good, because after all it only forms par of a syllabus with other works of English writing by people outside Africa. We certainly should also include in this, writings by white Africans like those in South Africa, Nadine Gordimer, Jack Cope, Alan Paton, and Dan Jacobson; also Joyce Carey, Joseph Conrad, Elspeth Huxley, Doris Lessing: these are artists who should be introduced into university teaching so that the African student should be acquainted with the image of Africa as represented by Africans, white Africans and black Africans and non-Africans who are writing out of the African experience. So already, you see, we have quite a big body of literature to introduce as part of the university syllabus which as I say will also contain English writing by non-Africans.

The next interview was made with Robert Serumaga in December 1964, in Nairobi and used as a Transcription Centre Programme in 1965. The programme format is retained here, with the narrator's introduction and link. At the time of the interview, Mphahlele had recently gone to Kenya – to teach and to help set up the Chemchemi Cultural Centre.

NARRATOR Cultural revival in Africa made a further advance with the creation of the Chemchemi Cultural Centre in Nairobi, Kenya. Chemchemi is the Swahili word for 'fountain' and the centre is intended to be an East African counterpart of the Mbari writers' and artists' clubs in Nigeria. Ezekiel Mphahlele, the well-known South African writer who runs this centre, describes it as 'a symbol of freshness like that of a spring, a symbol of rebirth, and a springing forth of creative talent'. He told Robert Serumaga, who recently visited the centre, that Chemchemi is primarily concerned with four main themes of cultural activity: theatre, music, creative writing and painting and sculpture. As to how successful the centre has been so far, and what co-operation it was getting from government authorities, Mr Mphahlele said:

MPHAHLELE There isn't government co-operation in the official sense, but there are members of government who are personally, individually, interested in what we are doing and are encouraging us; they give us moral courage. We do co-operate very closely with the Minister of Education, because as far as writing is concerned, we are trying to stimulate creative writing in secondary schools. This means I often have to visit several schools and talk to pupils in the upper forms of high school on creative writing and on the various techniques, and we run a writers' workshop permanently which also does this outside school. We have now, so far, two hundred and twenty members, paid-up members, who come in to Chemchemi in the various fields of activity that they carry on, and these are very gratifying; most of the members are Africans, there are a few Europeans and a few Indians, but they're mostly Africans.

NARRATOR African Cultural revival of course, also means a particular African bias in artistic expression. This is probably easy in a society which is practically all African, but Kenya, where Chemchemi is situated, is a multi-racial society, or at least aspires to be one. This, therefore, prompted Robert Serumaga's next question.

SERUMAGA What would you define as an African play or a Kenyan play apart from the context in which it is written? In other words, what will be the criterion for calling a writer an 'African writer' in Nairobi?

MPHAHLELE In Nairobi? Well, many people say they foresee an integrated society, but at the moment I just can't see it, it is probably something in the distant future. The reason why I think so is because when people live a segregated life, they form their own ways of life, they create their own music, they create their own fun, they create their own place of entertainment, which is what the Africans have been doing, that's because they were cut off from institutions which are exclusively European. Whatever a man writes now, I think he'll not at all write as part of this integrated community at the moment: this is a thing of the distant future, as I say. So it means that a play, an African play will be one which draws on an African experience. Now this African experience would be quite varied. It could be exclusively African depending on whether the fellow, the writer, has lived in that segregated society; or it will bring in European characters, if he has had such an experience: but it will always reflect, his play will always reflect this kind of rift between the various racial groups. If there is going to be an integrated society, it's a long long way off. Come to think of it: with Africans now in power, they will want to assert the dominance of their own culture.

SERUMAGA   Now, if I may move on to another question. There has been a suggestion, by one or two artists in Kenya, that there should be some sort of institute of old African traditional sculpture and, in fact, they have gone as far as suggesting that traditional African sculpture is different from modern art in that they are two different streams. Now do you agree with this?

MPHAHLELE   Yes, they are two different streams. I don't see myself that there is any use in an institution as something that is only pre-occupied with traditional African culture; after all one thinks of culture as a movement forward and never a movement back, except only in individual styles, but we presuppose there is progress forward. This means that people have to create out of their own contemporary reality. It would be false I think if people tried to recreate old African sculpture, which was produced as a result of spiritual and religious impulses which don't exist today. That impulse is no more there, there is a new impulse and people create out of this impulse, and I think the best that can happen is that people should study their traditional sculpture – study it to get used to it, and live with it so that they can, one way or another, try to bridge the gap that is between these two streams.

SERUMAGA   And if I may ask a general question. What is your general assessment of the cultural life in Kenya today, the amount of success it has at the moment?

MPHAHLELE   Things are very much confused here, I think, confused because of the immediacy of the past which is the colonial past. There has been the emergency which has rocked people quite a lot. There has been the fact of colonization itself, where people, I think, have lost confidence in themselves, and, I think, also place an undue emphasis on things that shouldn't be emphasized. What I mean is, you find a number of people here who will say theoretically they would like to develop African culture or African music or African theatre and that kind of thing, but will not go out of their house, take a few steps to go to something that is specifically

African. I think it hasn't yet become a passion with them, it hasn't yet become much more than the words they say about it. I say confused also because there's so much disparity in the economic life of Europeans on the one hand and the economic life of the Africans on the other hand, and because of this people can't share very well ... can't enjoy together the same things. There are things which the people at the top will go to because they can afford it, there are people here who can't afford more than two shillings at the door in going to see any play or even the cinema, and this is the kind of state of confusion I am talking about. So that I think we have still got to get our focus, gradually come to focus – when? Who knows! I mean the economic life of the people will improve and therefore it will give them more opportunity to go to a number of things, and also it will diminish their sense of insecurity, which is quite a harassing thing, I think, in a segregated life of this kind.

At the time of the recording of this next interview with Cosmo Pieterse at the new studio of the Transcription Centre in Paddington Street, London, August 1968, Ezekiel Mphahlele was on his way from teaching at Denver University, to the University of Zambia at Lusaka.
His collection of short stories, *In Corner B*, had been published in East Africa.

PIETERSE Zeke, the first thing I'd like to ask is: the two years or so that you've been in the States, what kind of impression have they left with you?

MPHAHLELE Well, the United States certainly left a disturbing impression on me. One knew the number of things that go on in the country with regard to what is often called the Negro Question – race relations and all that; but one came into real close contact with it in the United States, and one realized that it was a pretty serious thing, something that the Americans would have to apply their minds to, sooner or later. They certainly are, but it's pretty fragmented, the way in which they apply themselves to the problem. And the impression the United States left on my mind really concerned the bigness of the whole race question in the country. The negro front itself is very fragmented. Each time you listen to one negro leader speak, you feel he is telling the truth and you feel he is talking sense. But if all the negro leaders from the various flanks of the negro front – from the various flanks of the negro revolution – if you put what they said together, and imagined that one person was saying all these things, you'd just think that he was being crazy because they can be very contradictory. But at the same time you feel whatever they say expresses the yearnings of their own people.

PIETERSE The one little element that I'd like to extract from this is the impact of all this on literature in the States. For instance, one hears of the political expression in terms of Black Power. To what extent are writers like LeRoy Jones not only symptomatic of, but perhaps representative of a literary movement in this direction.

MPHAHLELE LeRoy Jones certainly represents a new movement in the negro consciousness which expresses itself through poetry. You do not find it expressing itself in the fiction of the negro so much as in the poetry because, again I suppose poetry is probably the most direct kind of medium through which people express their deepest feelings. LeRoy Jones – now, there is quite a core of negro poets, young people who are writing poetry that glorifies blackness, and go on the slogan 'Black is Beautiful', and it's their poetry that is rejecting totally the white man's assumption that the negro wants to be like him or that the negro is aspiring to white culture; there's a good deal of it that's negating this kind of thing. It's a very vocal kind of poetry, it is a poetry that gets published in small little thin volumes of anything like fifteen to twenty poems by one writer, and there is a publishing house in Chicago that is publishing a lot of this kind of stuff, and it is a new kind of renaissance. We had the negro literary renaissance in the late nineteen-twenties and early thirties and we are again witnessing another renaissance which is very much more virile, very much more passionate than its predecessor.

PIETERSE One thing that strikes one is that perhaps one could draw a kind of parallel between this renaissance and something like negritude. Now in *The African Image* you are very concerned about the meaning of negritude and perhaps its negative qualities. To what extent would you have second thoughts on perhaps negritude, or first thoughts on the Black Power poetry, if one could call it that, which will to some extent qualify what you felt about negritude, or would you still feel that both are too negative?

MPHAHLELE I still feel that it depends really on the area of negritude one is talking about and I would not change my views at all, even now, because I still think that in the African context, negritude has overplayed itself and that negritude, purely as a cultural front against colonialism and white culture, is now something that has succeeded in what it set out to do, and now that the African is independent, and now that the African should be able to make his own choice, what he should adopt and what he should reject, I don't think that negritude is necessary. Again, we begin to realize now that the beginnings of negritude were after all in the Caribbean and in the Western Hemisphere generally, so negritude proper was an expression, the outcry of an alienated people, people who couldn't go back to Africa and recapture their African roots because they were complete exiles, and this is why negritude found its most poignant expression in this area: it was a natural beginning for negritude. But how different with the African: an African who feels alienated can always go back to Africa if he wants to, and if he has a mind to it; he can go back and recapture his roots and he *can* because, after all, a good deal of Africa is still very traditional, and all he needs to do is go back to his people and make the contact again, while the negro in America and the negro in the Caribbean could not do that. So we begin to realize, all the more now, that it is a Western Hemisphere negro phenomenon more than an African one. Because now, and I'm beginning to sympathize more and more with the American negro, because there is in their expression of Black Power a negritude, because they are culturally in a state of siege, they are besieged by a formidable white culture which is threatening to suck them in, on its own terms; and the African is not in this situation at all. He is not in a state of siege; and I do certainly sympathize with this agony on the part of the negro, at the same time recognizing that he wants political and economic integration in America; he wants economic and political integration and he has – to do these – he has to fulfil these desires which he feels without compromising his own negro self which he feels. And then again the people who feel this really are more the enlightened kind of *élite* negro who feels this more than the large masses of the negro population. The Southern negro, for instance, who's never forgotten he's a negro, has never had a chance to forget he's a negro because he is even politically besieged by whites and oppressed so that he takes it for granted. It is this negro who feels threatened, who feels that he has been uprooted from his negro self, who feels that he has now to begin to protect himself against further assimilation, and this is the kind of negro we are dealing with who are represented by the new literary renaissance movement.

PIETERSE   And this renaissance to a large extent bases itself on the social and political realities of the American situation. Whereas negritude to some extent romanticized ...

MPHAHLELE   Romanticizes the past. It romanticizes the past, it is a yearning for the past, and a past which has gone, which has long gone. The negro at the moment in America is a synthetic human being, made up of so many impressions and so many cultures. I still think that he will continue to remain a negro, for the simple reason that negroes tend to gravitate towards one another in America. Wherever they are in social life, they tend to group together. You don't find them very often in places of entertainment where most white people go, they still remain a caste by themselves as a group an ethnic group; and it looks as if this is going to perpetuate itself and it's going to make them feel it's all the more necessary and even more natural that they should remain culturally exclusive, even though they're politically and economically integrated.

PIETERSE Could we possibly veer off a slight bit. I was struck by the phrase you used – a 'synthetic person' in the sense of somebody who complements in himself a number of different cultures. Now to a large extent this seems to be the kind of pattern that one will have in Africa. There is a lot of literature that comes from the West, there's a lot of the new literature that is being produced in Africa, there's a lot of work to be done in digging out the real old traditional literature.

MPHAHLELE Yes, the real old, the real traditional literature. We are dealing in Africa with a number of forms which are alien to Africa. Although we have told stories in the oral tradition before, for centuries, the novel itself is a new medium to Africa. The novel as an individual occupation, as an individual craft where you require an individual to sit down consciously and compose something, in a form which also after all is a bourgeois form, it's a middle-class medium, the novel. Well, then, it is a new thing in Africa. Now, when we adopt the novel as a medium of literary expression, we are writing in a tradition which already exists, that tradition of the novel in the Western world, and we are trying to write about Africa, give an expression to something African through a foreign medium. This creates a number of problems, problems in style and problems in content and problems in the structure of what you want to say. Now there are people like Tutuola, who naturally write what they do without deliberately doing so – Tutuola is not a conscious artist at all, he is just telling stories, and you can see from his novels, particularly those following after *Palmwine Drinkard* they are more epics than novels, because he can go on and on and on and on, and the story goes on and there is no definite beginning and definite ending right? But this is unconscious, something that is not deliberate. Now the conscious artist still finds that he writes a novel that has been written before, only he is talking about Africa. Poetry, right, this is something that is traditional in Africa, but we are again introducing a modification and a partial determinant of form in using the English language. I think this is necessary, and I don't myself want to spend sleepless nights weeping over the fact that we are writing things in English or in French and not in our African languages. People who want to express themselves don't spend that much time trying to debate in themselves whether they should write in their mother tongue or not – they just write because the impulse is there...

PIETERSE In the mother tongue or in any other language?

MPHAHLELE In the mother tongue or in any other language, and once the impulse gives you the kick you just go ahead and do what you want and say what you want to say. Maybe it'll help a lot, as African scholars continue to probe traditional literature and get them out as it were, and record them, maybe it'll help. But I seem to think myself that there's going to be a wide gap, for a long time between oral literature, traditional literature and modern African literature.

PIETERSE I was wondering whether there are not a few pointers towards a bridging of the gap in things like *Song of Lawino*,* perhaps in the plays of John Pepper Clark and some of the recent plays of Wole Soyinka† and I was struck by a short story by somebody called Ezekiel Mphahlele, called *A Ballad of Oyo* which has a very singular, very particular kind of grace about it, linking the short story form with the almost poetic form.

MPHAHLELE That's right. That's what I was trying to do, and I quite agree with you, Cosmo, that there are signs that we are beginning to bridge the gap. It'll remain wide for some time but I think there are certain connections coming up and what I tried to do in the *A Ballad of Oyo* is: I thought of the ballad as a form nearest to the African story telling which is repetitive and an almost sing-song kind of thing and I said to myself, why can't a man tell a story in prose in this kind of fashion, and so I tried it out for what it was worth. And *Song of Lawino* certainly, I agree is one such experiment and perhaps what we're going to do, we're going to find that we are breaking down or doing violence to both traditions in these new forms. We may even do that to the novel, who knows, but certainly in poetry and in drama we're going to do that. I still think that maybe the drama that does this more than Clark and Soyinka is the drama that is being written to be performed on the spot. Like the things that are being done for the travelling theatre in Africa, in Uganda, in Zambia, in Dar-es-Salaam in Tanzania, in Ghana and so on. It seems to me that these are the ones that are coming right across to the people immediately. Because I think when you look at Clark and Soyinka at least in their earlier plays, their first plays, you will find it's still determined by the conventional proscenium arch theatre. You've got to have a stage and everything done within this kind of framework. This apart from the style and from the

* By Okot p'Bitek, for whose interview see p. 149.
† For interviews see pp. 63–74 and 169–180.

diction. But in terms of structure and form we need to break away from that, even in terms of the plays we actually write which are going to be read. And I would like to see – I think we're going to see – more and more of this kind of new theatre building up in Africa. That will be one very good transition point.

PIETERSE   It does strike me that for instance in *Ozidi*, the latest Clark play, there is a development . . .

MPHAHLELE   There lies a development in that direction, you're quite right.

PIETERSE   I was wondering to what extent would this be happening in your short stories more and more: I think of *He and the Cat* which has a lot of what one might call the modern short story – modern novel form, the objectivity, and yet at the same time there is a trend, there's a kind of 'texture' that doesn't seem to be altogether 'Western', but this applies, it seems to me, to almost every one of the stories in *In Corner B*. But to just break away from that altogether, Zeke, I was wondering what has happened to your older collections of short stories: are there some that you'd like to resuscitate, is there a likelihood of them being issued again by the publishers.

MPHAHLELE   My first volume which was *Man Must Live* of which only the title story appears in *In Corner B* was the very first one, and it was a clumsy piece of writing I felt, and is something that I wouldn't want to read again.

PIETERSE   You don't think other people might want to read it again?

MPHAHLELE   No, I don't think other people – well they probably want to do it out of sheer curiosity.

PIETERSE   To trace the development. . . .

MPHAHLELE   . . . to trace the development, ja, that's it, but I've moved quite a long way from there. When I wrote a story like *The Doorn Vlei Story*, I began to realize that I was doing something quite different from what appeared in *Man Must Live*, and the stories that I subsequently wrote for *Drum* magazine which were a series of stories with one setting, Newclare, in Johannesburg, with one family going through each story but each story quite complete in itself; I thought here again I was doing something quite new which I hadn't done before. Those are the ones *I* would really like to resuscitate: the ones that began somewhere in 1955 and from then onwards, those are the ones I *would* like to see if I can publish them, even if they were only as a string of sketches on some segment of South African life I would still want that to appear, but certainly not *Man Must Live*. The story that you see in *In Corner B*, 'The Coffee Coloured Girl', this is one of the first ones that appeared in *Drum* magazine, around 1955 and I felt this is the kind of thing I would want to bring up again and bring to light again in book form.

PIETERSE Zeke, could I just pick up this question of magazines: *Drum* magazine seems to have been one of the almost formative elements in writing in South Africa. To what extent can magazines like *Transition*, *Black Orpheus*, and especially magazines that are established say in the States or in England, help in the development of this growing African literature?

MPHAHLELE Growing, yes, they can do very much. I was invited recently by *Kenyon Review* which is published by Kenyon College in Ohio; they have contributors including people like Nadine Gordimer and other world-known short story writers. They are running a symposium on the short story and its future: the short story – what is becoming of it; and I made bold to say that in Africa I felt it was going to continue to be a viable medium. And it seems to me that journals like these can do a tremendous amount of good to the African writer who is either becoming apprenticed or who still wants to go back to, who wants to continue writing the short story. I am never satisfied myself with extracts from novels which appear in magazines, it just never seems to make sense to me; but short stories and sketches – that kind of thing should continue. The BBC, too, which continues to broadcast short stories from Africa is going to be a tremendous medium for Africans to be able to use. Which brings back the oral thing, the thing that you can listen to by ear. And I think, for radio, Africans will want to write something in terms of which they think of their audience much more closely as a literate or semi-literate and illiterate audience who just sit there and listen. I would want to see representative journals in Africa: you have *Black Orpheus* for West Africa and you have *Transition* down in East Africa; now, even though they circulate widely, we still have problems of communication and transport and it would be a good thing to see a magazine come up, say in Zambia . . . We've got the *Classic* in Johannesburg which manages to totter on in the situation in which it is, it operates. Well, we must have these magazines just pushing on and giving writers a platform, and people are not going to start writing I think, until they know that something of theirs is going to be published. That's right.

PIETERSE A bit earlier I mentioned, more or less in one breath, magazines which are published in Africa with those that are published abroad. Do you think there's any real demarcation between them. Might there be a danger, for instance, in journals like the *Journal of the New African Literature and the Arts* and *African Arts* and *Africa Today*, that they might be orientated towards a Western audience? Or do you think there are enough people with sufficient background in Africa, people like

Okpaku and Povey who know the field and are presenting African literature rather than trying ...

MPHAHLELE   I see, rather than trying to write something for an extra-African market. I think myself that once you've got people like those one can rely on, one can rest assured, I think, that they are good enough judges to know what sort of thing should go into these magazines which is not just a kind of slick, addressing of oneself to a Western public. I think it depends on the editor and I think we have in Povey and Okpaku, and we have in the editors of *Africa Today*, people who have been in contact with Africa for quite a long time, and are following the various changes in sensibility in Africa, and know what they should publish. Certainly with *Africa Today* the purpose is primarily to inform the Americans about Africa. We don't publish fiction yet in *Africa Today*. But those which are specifically for creative writing will do a good job and we couldn't have too many of them.

PIETERSE   There's one other thing that I was going to mention. It's again flowing from what you said: *Classic* in Johannesburg, *Transition* in East Africa and Mbari Publications in West Africa. There seems to be a trend towards regionalizing. Is there at the same time a trend towards giving an overall picture, do you think that this is done mainly by the extra-African publications?

MPHAHLELE   It seems so, that the extra-African publications will do more of that kind of work than the regional ones. *Black Orpheus* has tried right from the beginning not to be regional and *Transition*, too, although it started to be regional has now become bigger and solicits a good deal of material from other parts of Africa. Once these magazines go out more and more to get material outside their own regions, then we'll have something bigger going; and then take the extra-African ones which will give an overall picture of what goes on in Africa, in the African literary scene, we have something here to complement what goes on in Africa. And after all particularly a literary cultural magazine must depend more and more on Africa-wide material rather than regional material and also on an Africa-wide audience, and I think we see something here developing which is going to be a tremendous force in the African literary revolution.

PIETERSE   At the same time there are magazines like *Zuka* in Kenya which have both English and Swahili material. To what extent do you think this would be a very happy development in other countries, say for instance, if *Black Orpheus* or something like *Black Orpheus* were to give Yoruba and Ibo and Hausa material alongside, or would it be happier to some extent to keep the two literatures separate?

MPHAHLELE   I have always wondered about this. I don't have my mind clear about it yet, and I don't have a definite answer. But I have always doubted the advisability of having a bilingual magazine unless you're doing it in French and English; but English and an African language or French and an African language, I have often doubted the advisability of this, but as I say I am not yet really sure in my mind whether it should be that way or not, because what happens: it splits your readership. And it means you can only have a limited amount of Swahili material, a limited amount of English material and you have only a very small audience either side.

PIETERSE Except that perhaps in these cases, most of these magazines want to be regional and want to be specifically, let's say, for the particular area...

MPHAHLELE Yes, that's probable... yes. But I don't see any harm, for instance, in having a Swahili magazine, that'd be a very good thing for a thing like that to happen. Particularly because Swahili has the fortunate position which is not enjoyed by most other African languages, in that you have a whole big region speaking Swahili, rather than just a single country. And I think it could exploit that and have a really first-class Swahili magazine.

PIETERSE Do you mind if we switch a slight bit and deal with your programme for the immediate future, both academic and creative. To what extent do you think you're going to go on writing poetry – I've seen a number of interesting poems also under the name of Ezekiel Mphahlele, is this a...

MPHAHLELE No, this is really playing around with things and I write poetry when I have nothing else to do. It's not something I want to do because I don't regard myself as a poet at all. I write occasional poetry and I think it's pretty bad because I don't trust myself...

PIETERSE May I quickly disagree. The one poem I've seen was a tremendously interesting one.

MPHAHLELE Well, thanks a lot, Cosmo, for saying that, but I'm pretty shaky in the poetry medium. I have a number of ideas running around in my mind, as you might say, almost in poetic form; but writing it down, I find my enthusiasm flags and I do it out of sheer compulsion sometimes. Maybe just a kind of vanity in me that tells me that I have to try to turn out something. But I don't want to flog away at it if I don't feel happy about what I'm producing. There are probably just a few things I'm happy about. In most cases it depresses me a lot.

PIETERSE The writing of the poetry?

MPHAHLELE The writing of the poetry...

PIETERSE It means that it's really the Muse working away at you!

MPHAHLELE I suppose so.

PIETERSE   On the other hand, in the prose field, the short stories, is there anything like a novel. One sees almost a tiny bit of a novel wanting to develop (not that it's not a complete short story), in a story like 'Mrs, Plum'. And perhaps again in 'Grieg on a Stolen Piano', it seems to have the dimensions or the potential. Is there anything like a novel developing anywhere? Have you felt like writing one, are you writing one?

MPHAHLELE   Yes when I wrote 'Mrs Plum' this was a kind of finger exercise to see what I could make of the long story or the novella, and once having done that I felt more confident; so I got into the novel and I have now finished a novel which is in the hands of the publishers, where I finished it, in Denver. This is my first attempt at a full-length novel and I think I'm going to do more of that. I'm not going to go back to the short story I think. I want to, I simply want to go on with the novel.

PIETERSE   Zeke, your short stories in *In Corner B* ingest the experience of South Africa and West Africa. What kind of experience is deployed in your novel if one may ask?

MPHAHLELE   It's set in three countries, South Africa, West Africa and East Africa and it's fictional in most cases; it's only autobiographical in the sense of the movement from one region to another, but what goes on in the body of the novel is highly fictional, the story-line itself. This is what I do: I travel my story in order to try to give, for me, for the first time, a kind of panoramic view of Africa and the torments that Africa is going through today.

PIETERSE   You mentioned 'autobiographical only in terms of the movement'. Well, I recall your autobiography *Down Second Avenue*, now with autobiography one wonders to what extent is recall quite objective or is there a kind of lyricism of recall that happens in the writing of an autobiography? To what extent do you feel that especially in the South African autobiographical writings there has been objectivity rather than lyricism?

MPHAHLELE   Rather than lyricism, yes; it seems to me that autobiography by its very nature has to consist of the elements you've mentioned. Romanticism and lyricism and fact, because one writes an autobiography at a certain point in his life far removed from his childhood and youth and you recall a number of things as far as you can; not all of them; and in some of them, with some of them you report as an adult sees them rather than as a child would have seen them even though they took place in the child phase of your life. And one simply cannot help doing this and there are a number of things that one becomes lyrical about in autobiography. The things that had made an impression on one's childhood mind, which stand out, now that one looks back, to them, stand out very vividly, and it's almost impossible to recall them as an adult would. Sometimes you recall them in impressionistic terms because you want to capture the atmosphere and the mood around which you can only, at best, project your mind back to, yes; and maybe there is no such thing as autobiography: maybe there is only autobiographical fiction or fictional autobiography in the final analysis. And that one is imagining a number of things and one is placing a number of things out of time and one only recaptures the general sequence of things, but how is one able to say he went to one place before he went to another. This is it.

PIETERSE But going from one place to the other, one tends to think of you almost as a man of three continents, the Americas, Africa and Europe. To what extent will these three continents do you think find reflection in the teaching of literature in Africa and in say other countries. One thinks for instance of centres like the University of California, of Stanford, of Denver, of Wisconsin, where there are big centres of African studies. Now in the literary courses for instance, say at the University of Zambia, where you're going, do you think one will have in the English courses English English, American English and African English literature?

MPHAHLELE Yes. Zambia is a very interesting experiment in this direction because the tendency in Zambia is to teach English literature according to the genre rather than according to periods. That is you say you are teaching the novel so you take a number of novels from various areas of fictional activity. You say then: 'I am teaching the novel so I'll have an American novel, I'll have an African novel, I'll have an English, a British novel and maybe even have an Indian novel in English.' What you're really doing is you're teaching the novel in English rather than the English novel, so this is how we do it. In the whole English course we have representative American, African, British literature, novel, poetry, drama, essays; and what we do is, in the first year we are teaching African literature because the student is being initiated into English literature and so it is best to do it via the African, via African literature, because it is a scene with which he is familiar. He doesn't have to project his mind into say *Northanger Abbey* or *Paradise Lost* – that sort of remote thing which they cannot identify themselves with – and I'm happy myself about this development: it does mean that we're going to grapple with literature as literature rather than the so painful, the really agonizing way we have been taught literature through the toughest kind of things you can imagine like Walter Scott and, again going back to Milton and Jane Austen, all those people.

PIETERSE Interesting writers, but sometimes a tiny bit far away . . .

MPHAHLELE Very far away, very far away and difficult to project one's mind into and I find I can just remember the agony I had trying to understand Walter Scott and trying to understand the classics generally in English literature.

PIETERSE   Zeke, I think this is going to be the final question. In a 'Guide to the Writing of ——' I think 'A Guide to Writing', a short little . . .

MPHAHLELE   Yes, *A Guide to Creative Writing*.

PIETERSE   *A Guide to Creative Writing* – in your foreword there's a little suggestion that pupils, students, writers, intending writers, should make a point of looking into the past or rather listening to the past, talk to the elders and listen to the stories and record them and tape them. One has had a lot of this happening, it seems, in Nigeria, and in Ghana. I think quite a lot of the poetry of George Awoonor Williams* gets all its richness from . . .

MPHAHLELE   From the language of the people.

PIETERSE   Precisely, now do you think a lot of this will be happening in literature departments of the Universities or will it be a kind of interdisciplinary thing, where say, a certain department like anthropology or sociology will deal with that and work across, cross-fertilize with the literature departments?

MPHAHLELE   Yes. I would hope this would happen. Whatever department feels it has the equipment in personnel and money to do this, should plunge into it without any further waste of time, and then have an interdisciplinary kind of process going on in the school. I would also hope that, say students of ethnology and students of literature themselves would do this as it is just so much part of the African life and literature: custom, law and the whole life of the African is so much mirrored in the literature, that I would hope this would happen in African universities.

* Kofi Awoonor.

John Nagenda
BORN 1938

▼▼▼▼▼▼▼▼▼▼▼▼▼▼▼▼▼▼▼▼▼▼▼▼▼▼

At the time of this 1962 interview with Lewis Nkosi at the African Writers' Conference at Makerere University, John Nagenda was working for Oxford University Press in Kenya. His short stories, poems and articles were appearing in the East African press and in magazines such as *Transition*.

Nagenda's articles, stories and poems for magazines in Africa, America, Europe and the United Kingdom have subsequently appeared in various books, collections and anthologies: *Origin East Africa*, ed. David Cook (Heinemann 1965), *Pan-African Short Stories*, ed. Neville Denny (Nelson 1965), *Young Commonwealth Poets*, ed. P. L. Brent (Heinemann 1965), *Commonwealth Poems of Today*, ed. Howard Sergeant (John Murray 1967) and *New Voices of the Commonwealth*, ed. Howard Sergeant (Evans 1968).

Nagenda is currently working on a number of literary projects including a children's book, a novel, a collection of his own stories, another collection of his poems, and a third collection – which he will edit – of stories by different African writers.

NKOSI John, as an East African writer, just what do you feel you've gained from this conference after you've been sitting there for about five days now?

NAGENDA Well, yes, that's true, sitting ... still, to me the first sort of gain is that I've made a lot of friends. So many people who have come to this conference have up to now been names: people who write, from all over Africa, and also one or two who came over from the United States. Well, they've just been names to me and it was very interesting to meet them in the flesh and to talk to them. And, of course, as we talked, as we discussed these many things featured on the conference agenda, it also enabled me to see what this writing is about and how to evaluate it. Also, as you probably know, the writing in East Africa could be much better, or shall I say, there could be much more writing in East Africa; well, it helps when you meet people who have already achieved something in the field of writing.

NKOSI Yes. So you feel that meeting these writers and talking about writing has helped you to orientate yourself in a certain direction towards your work.

NAGENDA Yes, only in the sense that we have done a bit of criticism for example and talked about particular passages. Now, probably there was a certain feeling in some writers that writing was easy: all you had to do was write about an African situation and you'd made it; all you needed do was get a publisher. But now comes a conference of this kind where everything was judged on a rigorous literary basis, and it stops one from being lazy. We haven't found one direction which we can follow, I mean any 'African' direction, because I do not believe there is such a thing but in as much as we have been able to criticize and judge what has been written by other people, it does help one to look back at one's work and decide whether one is satisfied with it or not.

NKOSI Yes. Now, having been through this experience of attending an African writers' conference, what did you feel were the shortcomings of this conference and what would you like to see improved in future conferences?

NAGENDA First one touches this very controversial issue of what is an African writer? I think, in other words: is it a person who is a black African, a negro African, or is it anybody writing in Africa, or is it anybody at all writing on African affairs? Personally, I think it's somebody who lives in Africa and who writes on matters which are also universal in the final instance, but which have got an African slant, in other words, which are based on the continent. I mean, for instance, the writing could be about Ghana, Nigeria, Uganda, but this is all in Africa, you see, and therefore I feel we could have profitably discussed writing by white Africans on African affairs, and this would have been a good thing, because we could have decided why it was different, or if it was different, and if it wasn't, why not. I think, therefore, that I would have wanted more in this kind of line.

NKOSI Yes, I see your point. You feel that white writers living in Africa, like Nadine Gordimer, Alan Paton and Elspeth Huxley, should have been invited to this conference?

NAGENDA Yes, or if they had not, I do feel that it would have been a good idea if we had discussed some of their writing. In a way, I see this conference as a pioneering work, therefore, perhaps, we could not have invited everybody. This was only a get-together to start things; but first, I think, even then, we could have discussed some of the writing of these people, even if they were not coming at all.

NKOSI What do you feel was the contribution of this conference to East Africa, having taken place right here in Makerere? Do you think that it would help in improving or stimulating literary activity in this area?

NAGENDA I think so, there are, oh, I don't know about five writers from this area and they will, I am sure, go back with their new ideas and with a new resolve to write more, and also the people who live around us who might not have come to this conference, have had their interest heightened by this conference, and we've carried material on this conference in the press, and on the air, and therefore, they ought to be in fact, more interested, and also there is one practical thing and that is that Ezekiel Mphahlele has suggested that we can set up a sort of 'Mbari' here, and this is a concrete aid to East African writing. So I think it has in fact helped East African writing.

The interview that follows was recorded in the Transcription Centre Studio in Dover Street, London, in May 1966, with Robert Serumaga. Nagenda had been on a tour to and in the United States in connection with his writing.

SERUMAGA John, where were you when you wrote these two poems? And what made you write them?

NAGENDA Well I wrote 'Flutes and Indians'* in Albuquerque, which is in New Mexico, and I wrote 'Storms' in New York. What made me write them? Well 'Storms' is perhaps the more personal poem, in the sense that I wrote it (as I said), in New York, when I was feeling quite depressed, whether because of New York or because of myself, I'm not quite sure, perhaps a combination of both, and I tried to write down a few of my feelings at the time, and the result was this poem 'Storms'. As for 'Flutes and Indians' I was flying from Los Angeles to Santa Fe, and we stopped in Albuquerque, which is deep in New Mexico, and used to be country inhabited – I suppose as all the Americas were, but Albuquerque perhaps even more so than some of the other areas – by Indians, and I had about forty-five minutes to kill in Albuquerque, I didn't want to go outside, but as I sat down in the airport which is rather small and dreary – a lot of flies and so on; a rather sordid place if I may say so – suddenly there was a bit of music, and also I could see blankets and other trinkets, you know, either made by Indians or supposedly Indian-made, and just the feeling of the

* Cf. *New Voices of the Commonwealth*, ed. Sergeant; pp. 178–9.

whole Indian question and so on came upon me quite powerfully. I think also because I had been dealing at that time with the negro question and the two are allied, because these are two people who have been persecuted in the Americas, in the United States, and I sat down right there in the airport and wrote it.

SERUMAGA   In your poem 'Storms', the first line is: 'The wind without is within me as well.' Now, is this poem 'Storms', a personal reaction to New York, is this wind just the wind of New York or in fact the wind of the universe without you?

NAGENDA   I suppose everything one does must have a part of the universe in it. In other words the winds of New York are also part of the winds of everywhere else, of London and of Kampala and so on, but when I wrote about it really, this was a particular testament, or particular confession of my feelings about New York at that time, and it was really both physical wind, because New York is full of these winds which roar through the streets, yes, it was that, as well as the moment of metaphysical wind, that whole question of New York and so on, and of the United States.

SERUMAGA   You talk about your 'thought-tossed and therefore thoughtless mind' and 'shreds of confusion' and things like this, and then you ask the question, 'And where is there an anchor against the buffets of this chaos?' Now, you as a poet, where would you think you would find this answer?

NAGENDA   A lot of different places: friends, you know, artistic pursuits, music and so forth. Again I suppose in the writing of a thing like this, for me just the act of writing down my thoughts is already sort of a way towards defining them, and therefore being able to master them in some way, and whatever the merits of this poem might be, and I think perhaps it's a bit too literary, I don't know, I quite like it because it explained what I was feeling. Whatever its merits, after I had written it down, I found that even though I hadn't been at peace, that suddenly because I had put down the thoughts, I was more at peace than I had been before I started writing it. So just the act of writing itself is a way of trying to find an anchor.

SERUMAGA   And talking about writing, how do you write these poems, do you work in concentrated moments of inspiration or do you sit and wait for the inspiration, or are you pushed towards writing by some sort of inspiration you just can't contain?

NAGENDA   I write a bit of poetry, mostly I write short stories and the rapportage sort of articles, but occasionally I write poetry. As for poetry, I can't sit down and make myself write, that is absolutely so, I get a particular feeling which is powerful, for me, and I must sit down and write it down. So I've never really tried to write poetry, to make myself conscientiously sit down and think up a poem. What sometimes does happen, is that a line might suddenly come into my head, a poetic line, and because I like it, and I don't write one line poetry as some people do, I then might sit down and try to sort of make a tail for this line, if you like to call it that, but otherwise I really wait for the inspiration to come, for the emotion; all my poems are emotional, rather than philosophical.

SERUMAGA Which one of these two poems do you like more than the other?

NAGENDA I'm in two minds about it: I like 'Flutes and Indians' because I think it's a cleaner, more sort of accomplished poem, and it hasn't got this overriding literariness which 'Storms' seems to have, but for me I'm nearer to 'Storms'; 'Storms' I wrote about myself and about my feelings, so did I of 'Flutes and Indians' obviously; but one is about people and how they affect me; another one is about myself and about how I affect me, you know . . . though, probably, it's 'Storms' I prefer. But I quite like them both.

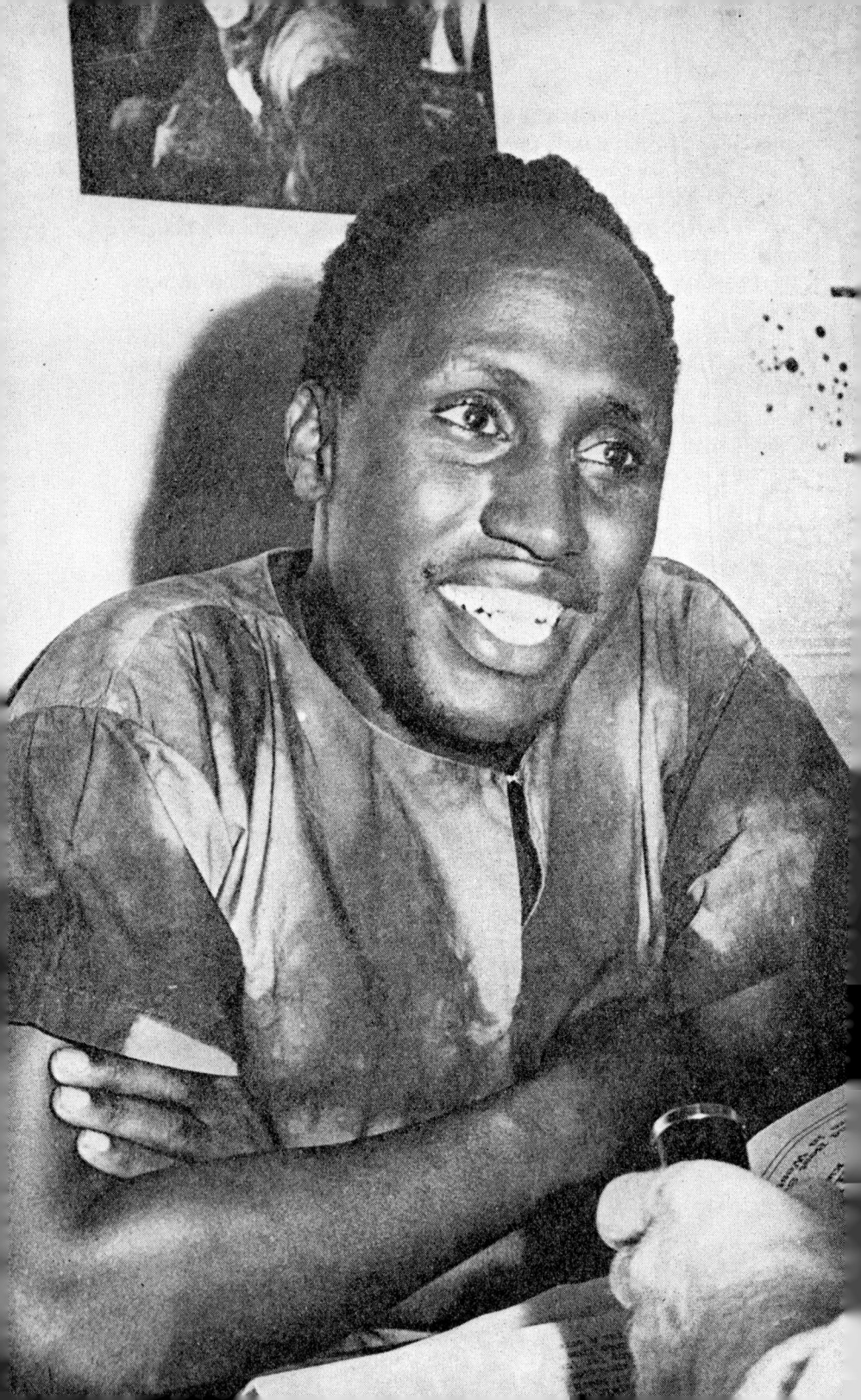

Ngugi wa Thiong'o
JAMES NGUGI
BORN 1938

▼▼▼▼▼▼▼▼▼▼▼▼▼▼▼▼▼▼▼▼▼▼▼▼▼▼▼

This interview with James Ngugi was made by Dennis Duerden in January 1964.
Ngugi had by then published in 1963 a play, *The Black Hermit*, in a small edition by Makerere University Press. This had been produced in November 1962 at the Uganda National Theatre as part of the Independence Celebrations in Kampala. In December 1970 his radio play, *This Time Tomorrow*, adapted for stage presentation, was published with two others by the East African Literature Bureau.
Stories of his had already appeared in *Penpoint* and *The New African* and stories, articles, and criticism were to appear widely in the next six or seven years. Some have now been collected and will be published as *Homecoming* (Heinemann, 1972).
In 1964 Ngugi had published his first novel, *Weep Not Child* (Heinemann) which is referred to in the following interview. Heinemann were subsequently to publish in 1965 and 1967 respectively, *The River Between* and *A Grain of Wheat*.

NGUGI   Actually in the novel I have tried to show the effect of the Mau Mau war on the ordinary man and woman who were left in the villages. I think the terrible thing about the Mau Mau war was the destruction of family life, the destruction of personal relationships. You found a friend betraying a friend, father suspicious of the son, a brother doubting the sincerity or the good intentions of a brother, and above all these things the terrible fear under which all these people lived. Some people in the novel, for instance, think that this is no ordinary calamity. That this, in fact, is the second coming of Christ. They go back to the Old Testament and the New Testament and they find that their fears are confirmed.

DUERDEN   Does this mean that your first novel is linked to your second novel, because I believe that the title of your second novel is *The Black Messiah*?*

* Cf. next interview, p. 125.

NGUGI In a way, yes, because *The Black Messiah* deals with a situation in the thirties when there was a clash between the Kikuyus and the missionaries and also between the Kikuyus and the government. The result of that is that we saw the beginnings of the political movement in Kenya and also the beginning of Kikuyu independent schools. Well, my second novel *The Black Messiah* deals with this clash; so in a way you might say that *Weep Not Child* is one more step after *The Black Messiah*. As a matter of fact, I wrote *The Black Messiah* first and *Weep Not Child* one year later.

DUERDEN When did you start writing? When would you say you first began work on *The Black Messiah*?

NGUGI I can't quite remember, but I think it was in March 1961. I was writing *The Black Messiah* for a novel writing competition which was organized by the East African Literature Bureau, the closing date was December 1961; and around January 1962 I began my second novel *Weep Not Child*.

DUERDEN What started you to write, have you always written or were you set off by the novel competition?

NGUGI I have not always written, but I have always been interested in writing. When I finished primary school, I was wondering why in fact people who were highly educated and knew the English language – I thought, for instance, that they knew everything about English! – could not write stories like those I read, e.g. by R. L. Stevenson. He is the one who really set my imagination flying and I thought that one day I would like to write stories like those which he himself had written. For instance, *Treasure Island* had made a big impression on me and I thought that if ever I got enough education I would like to write a story like that one. That was around 1955.

DUERDEN Can you talk about other writers, or other novels which have influenced you in your writing?

NGUGI When I went to Makerere in 1959 I was very much taken up with Peter Abrahams.* I found his stories very moving and I tried to read as many of his novels as I could, and then, just soon after Peter Abrahams, I discovered D. H. Lawrence, and again his way of entering into the spirit of things, as it were, influenced me quite a lot.

* By 1959, Abrahams had had published one book of stories *Dark Testament* (Allen & Unwin, 1942), five novels: *Song of the City* (D. Crisp, 1945), *Mine Boy* (Faber & Faber, 1954 – New York: Knopf 1955), *The Path of Thunder* (New York: Harper, 1948; Faber, 1952), *Wild Conquest* (New York: Harper, 1950; Faber, 1951) and *A Wreath for Udomo* (Faber, 1956; New York: Knopf, 1956) as well as *Return to Goli* (Faber, 1953) – impressions of Johannesburg and S. Africa on a visit after living abroad – and the autobiographical *Tell Freedom* (1954).

DUERDEN   Presumably you have read *Things Fall Apart*. At what part or time in your career would you say that this took place?

NGUGI   I think it was soon after D. H. Lawrence. I began ploughing into African writers and I began with, I think, yes, with Achebe – *Things Fall Apart*.

DUERDEN   So you had read a number of African writers before you started on your own work?

NGUGI   I think so, yes. I had read Chinua Achebe, I had read Ekwensi and I think some of the West Indian writers, and I think these people set my imagination flying.

DUERDEN   Would you say that you had two sets of influences, one from African writers and one from English writers, and if so, can you distinguish between them?

NGUGI   I do not think that I can easily distinguish between them. What the African writers did for me in a way that no other English writer could do for me was to make me feel that they were really speaking to me: the situation about which they were writing was one which was immediate to me, and also I found for the first time I was talking with my own people. I was talking with characters whom I knew, in a way, who had agonies which I had seen with our own people in Kenya and at that point I felt that if there could be Africans who could write such stories, I could write as well. I felt with D. H. Lawrence, although the situation, the geographical situation and even the moral situations he is writing about, are in some ways remote to me, that he is able to go into the spirit of things. You know I felt as if he was entering into the soul of the people, and not only of the people, but even of the land, of the countryside, of things like plants, of the atmosphere.

DUERDEN   This sort of theme of identification with land seems to be quite a strong one in your work. I mean somehow the relationship between the European farmer and the man he has replaced in this first novel of yours, which has been published, is somehow tied up with the land. Would you say that this was a principle, a preoccupation, or even a principal preoccupation of yours?

NGUGI   Not mine, but more of the people at home. I know that the land, the soil has got a lot of effect on the people who come to Kenya, those people who have lived in Kenya, both African and European – I do not know very much about the Asian community, but I think they are also affected by the land. It is more than the material; it is not just because of its economic possibilities, it is something almost akin to spiritual.

DUERDEN   I think it makes it easier to understand why you find this kind of kinship with Lawrence. I mean his sort of identification between the people and the land and some kind of natural forces. Would you say there are other European writers who have struck you in the same way?

NGUGI No, I wouldn't say in the same way. I know Conrad, whom at present I am reading, has, I think, affected me in a different way, but not because he is able to enter into the soul of things in the same way as D. H. Lawrence. When I am reading D. H. Lawrence, I feel the spirituality of things very near me as if I am touching the very spirit of things. With Conrad, I'm impressed by the way he questions things, requestions things like action, the morality of action, for instance.

DUERDEN Doesn't he question man's ability to have any control over his own destiny?

NGUGI No; yes and no, because while he questions man's ideas and man's ability to control his destiny, at the heart of Conrad is a feeling that man is great and reading Conrad one feels struck by man's capacity for bearing suffering, but much more than this, he questions what appears on the surface. He questions what I would call 'the morality of action'. What is 'success', for instance, what we would normally call success? What is 'action'? Is failure to make a decision a moral action or not? So you find that some characters in Conrad fail to do something, but their failure to do something is a moral decision with Conrad. This kind of questioning has impressed me a lot because with Conrad I have felt I have come into contact with another whose questioning to me is much more important than the answers which he gives.

The interview that follows was made in October 1964 with Aminu Abdullahi of Nigeria – then working as a script-writer, interviewer, and programme director for the Transcription Centre at Dover Street. Ngugi was doing a post-graduate degree in literature at Leeds University.

ABDULLAHI Mr Ngugi, your first novel *Weep Not Child*, which was published by Heinemann this year, was the first novel in English to be written by an East African. The theme of the novel is set against the background of the Mau Mau uprising. Well now, have you any idea what your next novel is going to be about?

NGUGI If I write another one – I'm not doing it now – but if I write another one it is going to be set against the emergency because the Kenya emergency or the Mau Mau war in Kenya is a very important factor in the creation of the present individuals in Kenya. It was a very formative factor in nation building.

ABDULLAHI   This reminds me of something that somebody told me – I think it was Mr Mphahlele – namely, that before *Weep Not Child*, you had already written a first novel, that in fact *Weep Not Child* was not your first book.

NGUGI   Yes, I had written what I then called *The Black Messiah*, which I have now changed to *The River Between*; it is being published by Heinemann, I think early next year.

ABDULLAHI   And what's the theme of that?

NGUGI   That one's set against the background of the clash between the Kikuyus of Kenya and the missionaries in the thirties. You know at that time, or about 1930 or so, Kikuyus quarrelled with the missionaries because of the circumcision of women.

ABDULLAHI   I see, and I believe this was the time when we had the first independent Kikuyu schools, as a result of this clash.

NGUGI   Yes, they clashed, some of the missionary churches would not allow boys and girls to go to their schools if their fathers had not renounced circumcision. So the Kikuyus, or a majority of the Kikuyus, sort of broke away from the churches and established their own churches and started their own independent schools run by the independent churches.

ABDULLAHI   I see. Why *The River Between* as a title for this work?

NGUGI   The river between: in the novel itself there is physically a river between two hills that house two communities which keep quarrelling but I maintain, you know, that the river between can be a factor which brings people together as well as being a factor of separation. It can both unite and separate.

ABDULLAHI   Quite. Incidentally, before you yourself started writing, were there any authors that made a particular impression on you?

NGUGI   Yes. I would say Peter Abrahams, not so much because of his style as the subject matter and he gave you the feeling that you also could write. After reading him, you felt that he also wanted us to go and write. I read Ekwensi, *People of the City*, and I read Chinua Achebe, *Things Fall Apart*, and all these writings were an inspiration, but of course from the body of English literature I also read quite a lot; I read especially Conrad.

ABDULLAHI   That's most interesting because I suppose English is not your first language. When did you first begin to speak English?

NGUGI   I first went to school in 1946 or '47; I started learning English four or five years later.

ABDULLAHI   I see. At what age would that be? About?

NGUGI   Thirteen, fourteen, fifteen, thereabouts.

ABDULLAHI   I see, I asked this because Conrad himself was not English-speaking until he was an adult.

NGUGI   Well, I understand he knew his first word of English at nineteen; that may be an exaggeration but I think what is interesting about Conrad is this very factor: that he was able to beat a language which was not his own into various shapes to give . . . well . . . meaning to the physical and moral world around him.

ABDULLAHI   Quite. One other thing. I wonder if you ever read Mugo Gatheru's book, *A Child of Two Worlds*?*

NGUGI   Yes, I read it: it's thrilling, in its own way: a straightforward account of the experiences of a Kikuyu searching for education; in fact, probably, the title should have been 'A Fight for Education'. I think it is important because of this very quality, this quality of fighting in the Kikuyu; you know that schools have always associated education with advancement, with political freedom, with even economic freedom. They have always seen education as a means to greater prosperity, and when the white man came to Kenya, and took away the land and ruled the people, they said to themselves: 'The white man can do this because he has got education, now if we also can get education, then we can get the things which he has.'

ABDULLAHI   I see. Now then, Mr Ngugi, coming back to Mugo Gatheru's *Child of Two Worlds*, I wonder if you could tell me what sort of reaction it received in Kenya?

NGUGI   I don't know what reaction it received from Kenya, because I think it was not extensively reviewed in Kenya,† and it's a pity actually it wasn't because I think it's a very important book. Certain qualities do emerge from the book, for instance the quality of endurance, the quality of perseverance and more: this fight for education is a classic example, the Kikuyus fight for education generally. I know one person whom I met, who after reading Gatheru's book said, 'This is just like me'.

ABDULLAHI   But this was also, as far as I can recall, this was the first time that an African had sat down and become absolutely frank about the most intimate details of his tribal background.

NGUGI   Oh no! Not exactly: Kenyatta's book *Facing Mount Kenya* I think of as going into Kikuyu rituals much more. . . .

---

* New York: Praeger, 1964. London: Routledge & Kegan Paul, 1964. Heinemann (A.W.S. No. 20), 1966.

† We have been able to trace no Kenyan reviews, only one in Britain (*Times Literary Supplement*, March 1964) and one in the U.S.A. (*Africa Report*, October 1965).

ABDULLAHI Well, perhaps I was talking about people of our generation?

NGUGI Oh, I see. Yes, certainly he's the first of the new generation.

ABDULLAHI Incidentally, now that we have you and Mugo Gatheru writing in English, do you foresee the possibility of having an East African school of literature?

NGUGI Well, I wouldn't use the word school exactly but I would say that what has been done in East Africa so far is bound to have an effect on the oncoming writers, it's bound to encourage a few people in their endeavours, and I know at present there are a few people in Kenya who are doing a lot of short stories actually.

ABDULLAHI I see. To what extent does the Chemchemi centre which is being run by Mr Ezekiel Mphahlele help in this way?

NGUGI This Chemchemi is playing a very important role in the creation of literature in Kenya, or in East Africa generally. For instance, Chemchemi has been holding exhibitions of African artists, and then you get very many African people in Nairobi asking, 'When is the next exhibition?' It is one of the interesting features about Chemchemi because normally you just say that Africans don't like art and so on, but many of them are going to Chemchemi, and to see what is happening there could belie this kind of general comment.

ABDULLAHI Quite. I understand that you gave some lectures to one or two classes at Chemchemi. What were the lectures about?

NGUGI Chemchemi has also been holding a writers workshop; this is being attended by people who hope to or are writing fiction, short stories, novels and so on, and I only talked to them once about the problems of the African writer.

ABDULLAHI What would you say are those problems?

NGUGI Well, I told them that I thought the problem of the African writer was actually himself.

ABDULLAHI But surely this is a problem with any writer, whether he is an American, a Pole, or a Chilean.

NGUGI Precisely, that is the point I was trying to make, but in the African context or in the Kenyan context, the geographical or racial situation adds a special problem which makes it even more difficult for the African writer to really confess what's in his heart of hearts.

ABDULLAHI I see. A little while ago you mentioned the fact that you had read Ekwensi and Achebe; now then, I wouldn't have thought that Achebe in particular had this problem.

NGUGI I should have been more particular and said in Kenya, where we have got three communities: we have got Asians, we have got Africans and we have got Europeans and you know the history of Kenya has been one of racial tensions, racial quarrels: one of African people feeling they have been rejected, or feeling they have been subjugated to a certain class or position. Now the problem with the African writer in Kenya is surely one of being able to stand a little bit detached; and see the problem, the human problem, the human relationship in its proper perspective.

ABDULLAHI   Well, what is he supposed to do then, stand outside of the problem and write purely as a spectator and observer, or else . . . ?

NGUGI   Not exactly. I wouldn't use the word 'observer' plain and simple. He has got to be an observer, and at the same time a part of him is committed, committed to the situation. Let me put it this way: he must be wholly involved in the problems of Kenya; at the same time he mustn't allow the involvement in that particular social situation to impinge on his judgement or on his creative activities. A little while ago I talked about confession, let me now say a little bit about it. Writing, I take to be a kind of confession where the writer is almost confessing his own private reactions to various individuals, to various problems, you know the feeling of shame here, the feeling of inadequacy there, the love-hatred. But in a place like Kenya you might feel inclined to want to say only the good things about your community and pass over the other communities because you see you are fighting for your community, and I tell you, this tendency is very, very strong indeed, after being in that place in your country, you know, you might feel compelled to want to justify your position and your people, and only say the good things about them. Or necessarily take the other communities as mere illustrations of an attitude; when you take these characters from the Asian community, or the European community you might tend to use them as mere pieces of wood.

ABDULLAHI   I see. This is most interesting. Now you are here to read literature at Leeds University. What particular branch of literature do you particularly want to concentrate on?

NGUGI   I am hoping that I may be able to do something on West Indian literature. Probably this sounds strange.

ABDULLAHI   No it doesn't. I can see the reason why. For instance the West Indies is also a mixed community.

NGUGI   Yes. The West Indies is a mixed community, and also the literature is just emerging, and there would be interesting parallels and contrasts and comparisons between this emergent West Indian literature and the new literature from Africa.

ABDULLAHI   What sort of writers from the Caribbean do you particularly enjoy reading?

NGUGI   I must confess I have not read very many, simply because their books are not available in Kenya, but I was overwhelmed by George Lamming. I read him uncritically – almost everything he wrote, uncritically – from cover to cover. He really overwhelmed me. The other person whom I like is Naipaul.

ABDULLAHI But Naipaul insists that he must not be labelled as a West Indian writer. He claims that he is a writer, period, of no particular school. The mere fact that all of his works to date – excepting his latest book, *An Area of Darkness*, which is about his journey to India – all his previous efforts were based on or were set in the Caribbean, he claims, does not make him a West Indian writer.

NGUGI As far as he physically comes from the West Indies and the fact that he's written about West Indians and himself, he can't help but be a West Indian writer.

ABDULLAHI This is most interesting. To take up your other point, his best-known work *A House for Mr Biswas* is a good case to support the point you made earlier: that he has chosen the Indian community and painted them white and he has used other people in the West Indian community as pieces of wood to support some of the ideas he wanted to put forward.

NGUGI Yes. This is a great tendency from people who are writing from plural communities. I must say I don't blame him. I can explain them without excusing them. In a place like Kenya you really don't know about the other communities. You don't know how the children play, you don't know the talk that goes on at breakfast, at lunch-time, at night, you rarely meet on such occasions. You must officially meet at parties, but then people are normally quite official at parties. That is you do not know the European character in his own home, which is very important.

ABDULLAHI Quite. How long are you going to be in Leeds?

NGUGI About two years, I hope. I have been given a scholarship by the British Council, initially for one year but I am hoping that I may be able to get some further grant to stay for two years.

ABDULLAHI During your stay are you proposing to continue with your writing, or do you intend to solely devote your time to your academic work, and then take up creative writing later?

NGUGI I am expecting the two to exist side by side and live together! All my writing so far I did when I was at Makerere College in Uganda. Anyway, I see my intellectual activity as contributing towards my creative activity. So that when I am at Leeds I am hoping to write at least a novel and dive into the 'Kenya Emergency'.

ABDULLAHI I see, this promises to be a most interesting work. But, coming back to the West Indian writers, do you realize that all the established West Indian writers are in fact resident overseas, with one or two, or, at most, very few exceptions?

NGUGI   I understand so, though I have not met any of them so far. What, for me, is very important, is that I like reading them; I like George Lamming for instance.

ABDULLAHI   Well, for instance, Lamming: he has been in Britain for about nearly ten years now, and people like Dathorne are working in West Africa.

NGUGI   This does not upset me at all because they are not writing about their exile, they are writing about the West Indies, they are writing about human characters, about human relationships and as long as their stay away does not falsify their image, or does not falsify their writing, I am . . .

ABDULLAHI   Wouldn't you find it extremely difficult after being away for ten years. Supposing you were out of Kenya for ten years, and you base a novel on the Kenyan situation, surely there are bound to be certain areas where you have to draw on your imagination very hard?

NGUGI   I agree with you but it depends on the period in which you are writing. We don't know as yet how the quality of imagination works. The quality of the imagination is the synthetic factor which makes the work of art, it depends on the period, you know, whether your exile will falsify the image you make, would, I think, depend on the geographical and social situations you take. For instance if George Lamming were writing a book after ten years in Britain and away from the West Indies and he sets it in a social situation prevailing during his childhood somewhere in the West Indies, surely for me this seems to be quite good background material for his creative work. However, personally, I wouldn't want to stay away from Kenya for so long and still write about Kenya.

ABDULLAHI   Incidentally there is also another point to be taken into consideration. To most Africans, English is a second language, but with the West Indians it's their only language.

NGUGI   Yes, I think that's another interesting point because, yes, the African writer in fact has got this added problem, you've just reminded me of it, whereas people like George Lamming or an English English writer can get narrative value from the 'slang', from twists of language from his community; we have got to get the slangs and the twists of language in a different language and then try to put that into English. You have visited Kenya, not many Africans speak English anyway and even those who speak don't use it as their normal language. It is not what they use every day, at breakfast, lunch, when they make jokes and so you're getting nourishment, linguistic nourishment in a different medium and then trying to use the English medium to create.

ABDULLAHI Do you think first in Gikuyu and then transpose your thoughts into English, or do you first automatically write straightaway in English?

NGUGI I think I write straightaway . . . I think . . . I never really know what really happens, but I am not aware of thinking first in another language. I think when I come to write, I just write.

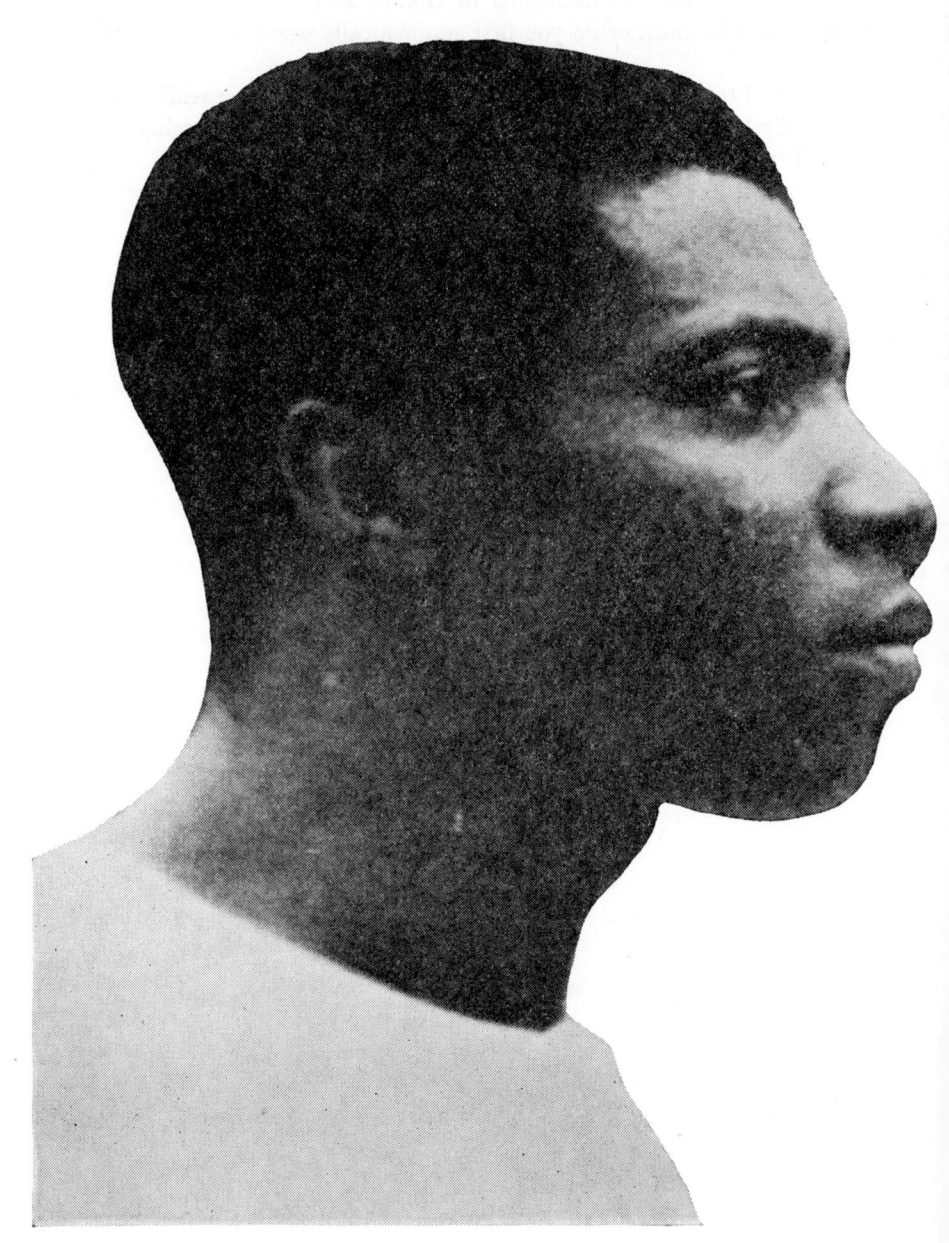

Christopher Okigbo
1932–1967
▼▼▼▼▼▼▼▼▼▼▼▼▼▼▼▼▼▼▼▼▼▼▼▼▼

At the time that Christopher Okigbo recorded the first interview – in Ibadan in August 1962 with Lewis Nkosi – he was the Cambridge University Press representative in Nigeria and Mbari had published *Heavensgate*, a volume of poetry. *Limits* (Mbari 1964) was to be the only other volume of Okigbo's verse to appear during the poet's lifetime.
A definitive edition of Okigbo's poetry, entitled *Labyrinths*, has been published by Heinemann in the African Writers Series.
In the meantime, poems or extracts from poem-sequences, are to be found scattered in numerous anthologies, magazines and collections: *Modern Poetry From Africa* (ed. G. Moore and U. Beier, Penguin); *African/English Literature* (ed. A. Tibble, Peter Owen); *A Book of African Verse* (ed. C. Wake and J. Reed, Heinemann); *Nouvelle Somme* (ed. L. S. Senghor, Présence Africaine); *West African Verse* (ed. D. Nwoga, Longman); *African Poetry* (ed. O. R. Osborne, Macmillan); *Our Poets Speak* (ed. D. St John-Parsons, Univ. of London Press).
'Distances', the fifth part of a much longer work entitled *Labyrinths* first appeared in *Transition* (No. 16, Nov./Dec. 1964) and then, with interesting variations, in Howard Sergeant's *New Voices of the Commonwealth* (Evans 1968). 'Dance of the Painted Maidens' was published in *Verse and Voice* (a festival of Commonwealth poetry) the Poetry Book Society publication for the 1965 Commonwealth Arts Festival, where Okigbo's 'Lament of the Drums' was also performed. Another version of 'Lament of the Drums' appears in Sergeant's *Commonwealth Poems of Today* (John Murray 1967) and yet another in *Black Orpheus* June 1965.
Reviews of Okigbo's work occur in *Black Orpheus*, No. 12, Ulli Beier on *Heavensgate*, and No. 15, O. R. Dathorne on *Limits*; and criticism in No. 20, Paul Theroux in 'Voices out of the Skull'. See also *Présence Africaine*, No. 66, pp. 49–57, *African Literature Today*, No. 1, 1968; Memorial poems to Okigbo occur in *Transition*, No. 35, Feb./March 1968. Also in *The Conch*, Vol. 1, No. 1, March 1969, which contained, in addition, an analysis of 'Distances'. Some of Okigbo's earliest poetry is published in *Black Orpheus* (No. 11, pp. 5–9); perhaps his very last

poems appear in the new edition (Feb. 1968) of *Black Orpheus* (Vol. 2, No. 1. pp. 5–11). 'Limits' first appeared in *Transition*, Vol. 2, No. 5. July/Aug. 1962.

NKOSI Chris, could you just say something about your collection of poems, *Limits*?

OKIGBO The limit is, I will say, the limit of a dream and the prelude* is about one-quarter of it divided into four parts, the first one which is the prelude to the preludes, and the second one which is a response by a chorus, the third one is the first development, and the fourth one is a divagation. Then we go into the heart of the work itself; there are six parts to the main work itself and the last one is almost an epilogue. But I do not think I can say very much about the *Limits*. They happened at the time they happened, and I do not know whether they could have happened at any other time. I wrote the first four parts, in other words, I first wrote the prelude and then there was a long gap of about three months before I did the other parts.

NKOSI How long did the whole work take you to write?

OKIGBO Oh, I would say it took – I wasn't working on it all the time but the prelude, the first part of the preludes I did early in August 1961, and I didn't complete the whole work until, I believe, sometime in May 1962.

NKOSI Is this the first collection of your poems that is going to be published?

OKIGBO No this is the title poem of the second volume which will be published.

NKOSI You have had poetry published before in book form?

OKIGBO Yes, I have *Heavensgate*, which is my first volume published by Mbari Publications.

NKOSI Who is publishing this latest volume you are working on?

OKIGBO It is also Mbari Publications. It will be coming off in October with drawings made by Susanne Wenger.

NKOSI I see. Have you been writing poetry long?

OKIGBO No, I wouldn't say so.

NKOSI When did you start?

OKIGBO I started writing poetry seriously in 1957. I mean everybody wrote poetry at one stage at school and at the university, but I didn't con-

---

* In some versions, the first four sections of *Limits* are entitled 'Prelude To The Limits'; in the Mbari publication they are called 'Siren Limits' and the last six parts 'Fragments out of the Deluge'.

sider that as something very serious. I did some translation from Latin verse to English verse and vice versa but I never really took poetry seriously until 1957, and the first poem I have preserved dates as far back as 1957.

NKOSI   Had you left the university then?

OKIGBO   Yes I had left – I left in 1956.

NKOSI   I see. What inspired you to begin to write? Were you interested in writing before?

OKIGBO   Yes, I was doing a lot of writing before. At school, I was editor of a house magazine. At the university in fact, I had my own newspaper *University Weekly*, which ran into trouble because I didn't have enough money to continue publishing it. But I don't know what inspired me to write poetry other than the fact that – in fact I just started writing poetry at the time, I don't know what inspired me, or what didn't inspire me.

NKOSI   What do you conceive of as your audience? Are there many people in Nigeria who read poetry by the young Nigerian poets?

OKIGBO   In the first place there are not many Nigerians who would read poetry and who would take delight in reading poetry, and there are very few Nigerians who would read poetry that appears difficult. Somehow, I believe I am writing for other poets all over the world to read and see whether they can share in my experience. I believe that the best in poetry has been said, at least for the chamber. Nowadays everything is done for the study and on the few occasions it steals out, I think it is to please, but not a large public. Applause itself is no longer in a necessary personal experience. I think poetry is at the best a mere gesture to stay within a close, closed society or to be liked by the other fellow, one's fellows – so that I don't know how many people would really like to read what I write, but I don't care for applause. I believe that poets anywhere would get hold of my poetry when and if it is published, and it may be possible for them to get something out of the original experience.

NKOSI   Yes, but when you say you don't care for applause, don't you mean that you don't care for the applause from the populace which doesn't really understand the kind of poetry that you write?

OKIGBO   No, because I found that in most cases when my poetry has been applauded, it has been applauded for the wrong reason. I don't think I have any ambition to become a very popular poet. I think I am just satisfied if a good deal of friends come by my work and get something out of it.

NKOSI   So you really mean that you care for applause from intelligent people like other poets . . .

OKIGBO   Well, if they applaud, I would be delighted that there are some people who think seriously of what I think seriously of. But I don't particularly care ... I write the thing and it is finished and I particularly would like other poets to get something out of it just as I get something out of the work of other poets, not because I am a poet, but because I think I did take sufficient trouble to go into the thing – to look at the work seriously.

NKOSI Yes. Chris, there is a circle of very exciting young writers in Nigeria at the moment: could you tell us something about this community; did you use to know each other at the university when most of you were at university, young people like Wole Soyinka, J. P. Clark, and other people who are writing at the moment?

OKIGBO Yes, I'd say some of us knew ourselves at the university, knew each other, one another, but some of us went before other people. Chinua Achebe, the author of *Things Fall Apart* and *No Longer at Ease*, was with me both at school and at the university. Wole Soyinka was with me at university and we also met at cricket matches when we were at school. Our schools used to play cricket matches against each other. And in fact when Wole made his first public appearance as a singer, I accompanied him at the piano, playing 'Amabola', and it was a gorgeous evening. I also accompanied Francisca Pereira, who is now a very well-known singer. I usually accompanied her regularly in musical concerts at U.C.I.*

NKOSI Well, has your interest in music completely vanished since you became a poet?

OKIGBO Well, I stopped writing music when I started writing poetry seriously, this is in fact what happened, but I just have to have an outlet every time, and I was writing music seriously up to 1956. I started writing poetry when I stopped writing music.

NKOSI What has happened to this community of writers now that you are all outside the university?

OKIGBO Well, that is what has given rise to Mbari. We all meet again at the activities organized by Mbari, the Writers' and Artists' Club at Ibadan.

NKOSI Do you approve of each other's works?

OKIGBO God forbid! Why should we? How can we approve of each other's work? I mean ...

NKOSI Well, I do not know whether the fact that you studied together means that you sort of pat each other on the back on what you are doing. Are there different schools for instance amongst you?

OKIGBO No, in fact, I think some of us – I think we are all doing different things. J. P. Clark writes poetry, Wole Soyinka writes poetry, and both of them also write well, but they write entirely different things. Wole

* University College, Ibadan.

laughs in his poetry, J. P.'s poetry is more serious, but J. P.'s poetry is quite different from mine and I believe we are doing different things. He has written some very good poems and some very bad poems, and probably I am one of his severe critics, and I think he is one of my greatest adversaries.

NKOSI I see, that is very interesting. So you do have some kind of literary disagreement?

OKIGBO Oh yes, we do – a great deal of it.

NKOSI Are you intending to write only poetry or do you want to write other things besides poetry?

OKIGBO At the moment I don't know. I was thinking of working on a novel and really did make a start, but I don't know whether I'll ever finish it or even if I finish, whether it will be worth reading. I think that probably I would continue writing poetry until I'm grown up completely, but I do work on other things, you see, when I am not writing poetry. As much as possible, I keep practising – I mean I try to keep informed. If I have nothing to say, I translate from Latin verse into English verse or from Greek verse into English verse and vice versa. I mean if I have nothing to say, I just keep translating – keep playing with work because I have seen that a poet, apart from being a writer, is also a technician. I mean I believe in this. I believe that there is an adage or proverb which says that there is a craft and it isn't just the art alone, there must be the craft. There is real carpentry also apart from the art, and *that* you have to keep practising. This one thing which gives me . . .

NKOSI So you don't believe in accidental poetry, if I may interrupt?

OKIGBO A poem can come by accident and a lot of it does come by accident, but it has to be moulded into the form in which you want it preserved and this means a lot of – this embraces the question of craftsmanship. I believe that there is craft apart from the art – if there is craft alone, then you can easily see through the thing and see that there isn't any feeling but art isn't enough, there must be craft also.

NKOSI Do you have a working knowledge of Greek and Latin?

OKIGBO Yes: in fact I think that I have a fairly *good* knowledge of Latin, a working knowledge of Greek.

NKOSI Enough to translate poetry from Greek to English?

OKIGBO Oh yes. In fact enough Latin to read and understand Latin poetry in the original, and understand before I translate – and in fact enough Greek to translate Greek poetry into English.

NKOSI What are your main influences in poetry, who influenced you most?

OKIGBO I think that what has influenced me most is not in fact poets, but the composers, the musical composers are the people who have influenced me more than poets.

NKOSI Yes. Could you tell us how this influence has worked on your poetry?

OKIGBO Well, it is very difficult for me to explain, but take 'Heavensgate': when I was working on 'Heavensgate', I was working under the spell of the impressionist composers Debussy, Caesar Franck, Ravel, and I think that, as in the music of these composers who write of a watery, shadowy, nebulous world, with the semitones of dream and the nuances of the rainbow, there isn't any clearly defined outline in my work: this is what happened in my 'Heavensgate'. As it stands now, there are parts of it I like very much, some parts of it I don't like but I preserve because – either because friends like it or because they just belong to the work and I really don't want to disrupt the work. I don't want to interfere with the created thing too much once it's done: I will let people pick what they like and leave the rest. Yes, I think that the musicians have influenced me much more than – well, of course, it is the same thing except that the composer is working in abstract form and the poet is working with words.

NKOSI Chris, at the Kampala conference that we attended, you said some very vile things about negritude poets, about Senghor* and other French-speaking African poets. Could you say what you dislike so much about negritude poetry?

OKIGBO It is not that I dislike it, it is because when you've read a lot of it you just hit through the whole pattern, you begin to have the feeling, or I begin to have the feeling that it is just like working a machine or, if you like, working a *duplicating* machine, you think that it is so easy to do. I don't know how much genuine feelings we have in a lot of negritude poems and the pity of it is that some of the negritude poets could still have been great poets in spite of negritude. I certainly like Senghor a great deal and I like a lot of him: I still believe that he has the loudest voice in Africa.

NKOSI Just to end this discussion, what do you feel is the greatest lack as far as the literary community in Nigeria is concerned? Amongst the young writers, for instance, what do you think you need most?

OKIGBO This is a very difficult question for me to answer because I would be able to say what *I* need most, but I would not know what other people need most.

NKOSI Yes, could you tell us about you?

OKIGBO What I need most is a more intelligent audience, that's all.

* Leopold Sédar Senghor, Senegal – cf. poems in Beier-Moore, Reed-Wake; poems and prose in Reed and Wake's Oxford Univ. Press 3 Crowns edition, and the poems of *Nocturnes*, translated by Reed and Wake (Heinemann, AWS 71).

At the time of the interview following (August 1963 - London, Dennis Duerden as interviewer) Christopher Okigbo was West African editor of the literary magazine, *Transition*, published from Kampala, Uganda.

DUERDEN   What do you conceive to be the separate roles of *Black Orpheus* and *Transition*?

OKIGBO   *Black Orpheus* with its insistence on blackness rather tends to picture a black mystique, what I call the black mystique – blackness for its own sake. *Transition* publishes anybody who cares to write for *Transition*, black or white. We do not discriminate. Our aim was to make it a first-class journal produced in Africa and we don't restrict ourselves to African contributors.

DUERDEN   Yes, I believe the original conception of *Black Orpheus* – the way that Ulli Beier conceived it – was as a place where African literature could be published.

OKIGBO   Yes, *if* it was only that, then there wouldn't be anything wrong with that but it is in fact sub-titled a 'journal of African and Afro-American literature' and any American who is dark can get published in *Black Orpheus* and I would still want to be convinced that there is the sort of strong cultural link, which Ulli Beier imagines exists between Africa and Afro-America, you know.

DUERDEN   Yes. I suppose that this does mean that it has a special attachment to negritude.

OKIGBO   Well, I don't know whether it is negritude, what I call the black mystique, this emphasis on blackness. It means anybody who is black now can write for *Black Orpheus* even though there might not in fact be any cultural meeting points between the various black peoples of the world, and this is what I think is basically wrong with *Black Orpheus*. In other words it would publish an American negro but it would not publish a white American.

DUERDEN   But doesn't this mean that it starts with the idea that there's some sort of specific mental attitude that characterizes someone who's black – and this is what negritude seems to be saying; that all black people have some specific mental attitude.

OKIGBO   I don't quite agree. I don't think this is what negritude seems to be saying. I think that negritude seems to be saying that black people who have somehow felt a sense of alienation are now looking for their roots, which I think is a perfectly legitimate thing to do. But this is what *I* think negritude is saying. I think too that on another side the political equivalent of negritude tends to assert an African personality.

DUERDEN But, don't you think then that the magazine which concerns itself with African-Afro-American literature is concerning itself with the literature of black people looking for their roots and that perhaps in this way is stimulating an African literature?

OKIGBO Possibly, yes. If it was African literature, but I have seen, so far, no affinity between African literature and negro American literature.

DUERDEN You mean they are both looking for different roots?

OKIGBO They are looking for different roots. I think that the American negro feels a sense of alienation but it isn't from his African roots. It is just that he finds himself in a society to which he doesn't belong, which is an entirely different thing, but in a society where he isn't accepted.

DUERDEN Yes, so that the African, the negritude for an African is a response to a colonialist situation, but for an American negro its ...

OKIGBO It's a reaction against discrimination.

DUERDEN Yes. Before we pass on back to *Transition* from *Black Orpheus*, can you say what you think about the last number of *Black Orpheus* which has just arrived in London, the number that has the winning entries for the African writers' competition in it?*

OKIGBO I find it interesting, but I found Michael Echeruo's* poetry a bit academic. I didn't find sufficient feeling in it. On the other hand, I found Dennis Brutus* a very sensitive poet. Well – a real poet, not just an academic versifier.

DUERDEN What did you think about the reproductions from the Oshogbo painting school?†

OKIGBO I think it was a disgrace. Just a big shame and I think that Ulli Beier's greatest problem is that of not being able to see – to find a distinction between art and crafts, and I think this is a very serious matter.

DUERDEN Can you explain that?

---

* *Black Orpheus* No. 12, contains two poems by Brutus ('Kneeling before you' and 'A Troubadour' – both published later in *Sirens Knuckles Boots*, as well as nine poems by M. J. C. Echeruo (Nigeria, b. 1937–) the poetry first-prize winner who published, under the imprint of Longman, *Mortality* (1968), containing in Part I, 'Debut', eight of those in *Black Orpheus*, viz. 'Debut', 'Sophia', 'They', 'Wedding', 'Melting-pot', 'Nocturne', 'Easter Penitence' and 'Outsider'.

† *Black Orpheus* No. 12. Between pp. 26 and 27, 8 plates in black and white, on glossy paper – showing reproductions of works by Afolabi (I and II), Akinola (III), Remi, (IV and V), James (VI) and Buraimoh (VII and VIII) – painters at the experimental art school in Oshogbo, Nigeria. Afolabi (Jacob) was responsible for some *Black Orpheus* lino cuts and cover designs, e.g. No. 15; Buraimoh artwork, e.g. using beads, has been internationally exhibited.

OKIGBO Well I think that there is some – that there is a great deal of difference between carving and sculpture, for instance, a carver is not naturally a sculptor, though a sculptor carves; you know that carving is just a technique – it is just a method and –

DUERDEN I don't quite see how that fits these paintings by people who never painted before.

OKIGBO Well, I didn't find it interesting you see as an experiment, because in the first place the reproductions were ugly. The paintings were ugly – just ugly.

DUERDEN But are you saying that a painter or a sculptor should acquire some craft before he should be seriously considered?

OKIGBO Oh yes, certainly. If somebody is going to give us a good picture, I mean the most important thing about a painting is that it should be beautiful and if it is going to be beautiful then the painter has to have some sense of rhythm. There must be ways in which his colours can combine to produce a beautiful effect. He must have a sense of design. He must arrange his subject in a way in which it becomes pleasing to the eye, and I just thought those reproductions were ugly.

DUERDEN How do you think they compare with reproductions that have been in *Black Orpheus* in the past because they do seem to be evidence of a particular bias in *Black Orpheus*. I'm thinking for example of the reproductions of Malangatana* and reproductions of sometime ago of work by psychotics and then I believe they've had work by – American primitives and people like that.

OKIGBO I think that there is a definite bias. I agree, for instance, some of the better exhibitions we've had at Mbari, at Ibadan, haven't been reproduced in *Black Orpheus*.

DUERDEN Such as, which would you?

OKIGBO Such as one Sudanese calligrapher.† He hasn't been reproduced in – I mean there was a short review, but we didn't have full-scale reproductions. Georgina Betts had an exhibition and Malcolm Betts also. It wasn't a very good exhibition but I thought it was worthy of reproducing. I think there is a definite bias. I think that Ulli Beier, who edits *Black Orpheus*, feels very strongly attracted to work that looks experimental. In a sense artists are continually experimenting but I don't

* Valente Malangatana, Mozambique; poet and painter. A few of his poems are in the Moore-Beier anthology; his paintings can be seen in black and white reproductions in *Black Orpheus*, No. 10.

† Ibrahim el Salahi, whose work was reproduced in *Black Orpheus* (No. 10) and discussed by Ulli Beier. Mbari also published a volume devoted to the work of this artist.

See also, *African Arts/Arts D'Afrique*, Vol. 1, No. 1. Autumn 1967.

think that one should feel strongly attracted to experiment actually for its own sake.

DUERDEN   Now if we go back from *Black Orpheus* to *Transition*, I take it that what emerges from this discussion is that *Transition* attempts to be a good journal, rather than a platform for —

OKIGBO   Anybody who is black. Yes!

DUERDEN   Yes, but at the same time, I take it, it is still trying to perform this role of assisting African literature.

OKIGBO   Yes, certainly, critically. We believe, you see, that the time has now come to question some of our prejudices, to ask ourselves, for instance, whether there is such a thing as African literature, what characteristics a body or work may exhibit that will entitle that body of work to be classified as African literature? What is a good African novel, for instance, what is an African painting, what is African art? These are broad issues which we hope to tackle; and what is a good poem in fact, what do we consider good poetry? What is a good play, I mean what constitutes African drama? These are issues we think we ought to clear before we can prepare the ground for literary authorship. And this is what we want to do in the critical supplement.

DUERDEN   Would you say that this then is the main intention of *Transition*: to ask the question, 'What is good African literature?'

OKIGBO   Yes. In other words to establish the criteria for judging good African literature.

DUERDEN   And how is this to be assisted by including things from outside Africa?

OKIGBO   In the critical supplement we are going to have essays devoted to topics on African literature, but in the main journal itself, you know, which is simply a journal produced in Africa, we are going to publish poetry, Africans, non-Africans, short stories by Africans, non-Africans, in other words anything that is good we receive because I mean ultimately all literature is one and we are trying to serve a public. We are offering something to a public which is varied. Some of our readers, our subscribers are English, some are French, some are Japanese. We are trying to offer them what we can and they'll select what they want.

DUERDEN   Do you find that you have any difficulty in communication in conferring with the editor in Kampala, Rajat Neogy?*

OKIGBO   Oh, yes; I mean, we exchange letters as often as we can, but

---

* Rajat Neogy, Ugandan born poet and editor of *Transition*; poems published in *Transition*, Sergeant's Commonwealth Anthologies. Has lived briefly in U.K., U.S.A., Europe and Ghana from where *Transition*, after being closed down in Uganda in 1968, has been restarted.

naturally it would be much better if we could confer once or twice a year We did meet last year. This year I do not know whether there is a possibility of our meeting. If funds are available for him to come down to West Africa again for a meeting, or for us to meet somewhere mid-way between East Africa and West Africa, it would just be ideal but I think that we ought to meet at least once a year and commune with each other, and see whether we are still agreed – as we were at the time the liaison was begun – about the cardinal things we are trying to propagate.

DUERDEN   Yes, at the moment, then, your principal role is to supply material from West Africa?

OKIGBO   And also to produce a West African edition. It is only that my friends and I in West Africa felt that instead of producing a West African edition of the paper in general, we should produce a critical supplement.

The next interview with Robert Serumaga was made in Dover Street during the Commonwealth Arts Festival in July 1965. One of the Festival's poetry readings featured, among others, Okigbo's 'Lament of the Drums'.

SERUMAGA   Chris, is 'Lament of the Drums' a poem you wrote?

OKIGBO   Well, I really don't think I can claim to have written it. All I did was to create the drums, and the drums said what they liked. Personally I don't believe that I am capable of saying what the drums have said in that first part: it's only the long funeral drums that are capable of saying it and they are capable of saying it only at that moment when they talk; then they've said it. They are not capable now or in the future of saying that. So, I don't think that I can claim to have written the poem; all I did was to cover the drums, and to create the situation in which the drums spoke what they spoke.

SERUMAGA   There is a feature in your poetry, specially in the choral poetry – which is the period now you are in, it seems to me – there is a feature of it which it's very difficult perhaps to understand using the intellect only, but when one reads it, one responds to it. How do you explain that?

OKIGBO   Well, because what we call, understanding – talking generally of the relationship between the poetry-reader and the poem itself – passes through a process of analysis, if you like, of the intellectual – there is an intellectual effort which one makes before one arrives at what one calls the meaning. Now I think it is possible to arrive at a response without passing through that process of intellectual analysis, and I think that if a poem can elicit a response, either in physical or emotional terms from an audience, the poem has succeeded. Personally I don't think that I have ever set out to communicate a meaning. It is enough that I try to communicate experience which I consider significant.

SERUMAGA   In other words your approach – what it does really is to make one feel and then understand, rather than make one understand and then feel? Is it?

OKIGBO   Probably that.

SERUMAGA   Well, before you came to this period of choral poetry, you were writing in a sort of personal vein, for example in your poem, 'Heavensgate'. What made you change from the personal to the choral?

OKIGBO   I don't think that we can call that a change, because when we talk of my changing from the personal to the choral, it looks as if I made some effort, a conscious effort, as if I had, in fact, designed it. There wasn't any such thing. I found myself as a poet being called upon to show a particular type of responsibility and 'Heavensgate' and 'Limits', and also 'Distances', are in fact the way I have responded to that call. They are, I think, poems that deal with intense, personal experience, and they are, as it were, my own way of responding to an intensely ritualistic experience.

SERUMAGA   There is, on the one hand, what you call ritualistic experience in many of your poems; also there are three themes, death, birth and reincarnation, and when one reads the images that you put in your poetry, one gets the impression (I think this is not a mistake), the impression that you are very close to the traditions of your own society, is this true?

OKIGBO   This is true. In fact, I think that it is a lot of nonsense talk all this we hear nowadays of men of two worlds. I belong, integrally, to my own society just as, I believe, I belong also integrally to some societies other than my own. The truth, of course, is that the modern African is no longer a product of an entirely indigenous culture. The modern sensibility which the modern African poet is trying to express, is by its very nature complex, and it is a complex of values, some of which are indigenous, some of which are exotic, some of which are traditional, some of which are modern. Some of these values we are talking about are Christian, some are non-Christian, and I think that anybody who thinks it is possible to express consistently only one line of values, indigenous or exotic, is probably being artificial.

SERUMAGA   Quite true. And I'd like to explore further your connection with traditional and non-traditional values. Is there anything particular in your life, in the society in which you live which would give you this particular benefit over others (as it seems to me) of being in communication with the traditions more than many people are?

OKIGBO   Well, my maternal grandfather was the head of a particular type of religion which is intimately connected with my village and since I am a reincarnation of my maternal grandfather, I carried this on, and I began to show them my responsibilities in that direction as soon as I grew up; and even when I went to secondary school, I had to take something out of my pocket-money regularly to send home to my grandmother for my maternal uncle who was, as it were, standing in for me until I should grow up to carry on the various periodic rites which were connected with the worship of this particular Deity. And my 'Heavensgate', is, in fact, designed to do that sort of thing – it is my own contribution to this.

SERUMAGA   Perhaps this is a pertinent question: does your being a Christian, conflict in any way, in your own mind, with your other duties in this other . . .

OKIGBO   Oh no, I think it is just a way of going to the same place by two different routes. You can now fly from Lagos to London via Rome, on your way back you can fly from London to Lagos via Barcelona. I don't think that there is any conflict. Personally I have never experienced any conflict whatsoever in this direction. I wear an Italian jacket – I'm not an Italian, I'm an African. I wear a tie and I'm very comfortable. I'm not wearing Nigerian dress – I'm not comfortable in Nigerian dress – it doesn't make me a non-Nigerian. This afternoon I ate lamb chops – tomorrow afternoon I may eat pounded yam at Nigeria House, and I would still enjoy it. It doesn't make me non-Nigerian, or more Nigerian!

SERUMAGA   Talking about your influences in the other direction, or from the other direction there is the non-African influence. From where did you draw these influences – of course granted that they have now been completely integrated into one personality – where did they come from?

OKIGBO   I think that I've been influenced by various literatures and cultures, right from Classical times to the present day, in English, Latin, Greek and a little French, a little Spanish, but I think that in fact the question of influence is a very complicated thing. One reads something and says, this might have been influenced by one person. It's often difficult to pin down an influence to a particular source. If those sources have become assimilated into the subject and have come together to form an integral whole it is very difficult to sort them out – to know where the Babylonian influence ends and the classical influence starts, and where the classical influence ends, and where, if you like, the modern influence starts. I have been influenced, generally, by Greek and Roman poets and writers and also by modern English, French, Spanish poets.

SERUMAGA You read classics at the University?

OKIGBO Yes.

SERUMAGA It is quite evident from your poetry that there is this influence. But you consider it now to be completely integrated into a whole?

OKIGBO It is in fact completely integrated. You know yourself that in my 'Lament of the Drums' there is a treatment of the theme of Palinurus. In one section they are identifying the feet of the personage for whom the drums are lamenting with the feet of Palinurus. In another section of 'Lament of the Drums' there is a variation on the theme of Ishtar's Lament for Tammuz. This is taken from a Babylonian myth. So that in 'Lament of the Drums' alone, we have both: the first part is influenced by the oral tradition in African poetry, because the first part is the drums' invocation – the drums invoking the various elements from which they are made; in the second part they enter their theme song and talk of 'Babylonian capture', they talk of martyrdom, and we remember Christ and Judas and the betrayal; and in the third part they go into the story of Palinurus; they come back in the fourth section, tired and exhausted from their long journey to Rome, and in the fifth section they end with a variation on Ishtar's Lament for Tammuz. So now we have the sort of thing I'm talking about. We have traditional elements, we have classical elements, we have Babylonian elements.

SERUMAGA But these, when you bring them together in a poem like this one, this is not a conscious attempt to bring them in by natural reaction to the environment.

OKIGBO In fact, the third part, dealing with Palinurus was written before the other parts, and there is a three months' gap separating that third part from the other parts. I wrote the third part and subtitled it 'Lament of the Mariner' and later the theme grew in me, after I had completed it, and I found that that mariner, for whom the flutes and the drums lamented in the third part, which was Palinurus, had grown also into a vegetation God – Tammuz.

SERUMAGA When we come back to the problem of communication: there is a question often raised about your poetry – that a poet should be able to give society a definite message. Do you agree with this?

OKIGBO It is difficult for me to answer 'yes' or 'no' because I can only answer in terms of my own work, because my own work should bear witness to what I believe. 'Heavensgate' and 'Limits' do not attempt to carry any message whatsoever. If anybody reads a message into them, all well and good. The poems have nothing to do with me, the poems live their own separate lives and when you've created a poem, written a poem it is just like creating something, I'm giving it life. It goes to one audience and speaks one language, goes to another person and speaks a different language – it may go to another person and remain mute and no message is delivered, so that when we talk in terms of communication, it is something that is a little complicated. 'Heavensgate' and 'Limits' – I didn't have any particular message in mind when I created the two of them. But since then I've started writing through other persons. When I created the drums all I did was to create the drums and the message they deliver has nothing to do with me at all. It just happens that there might be some political tinge in the message of the drums and also the message of the silent sisters* – there might also be some political tinge there – but the message has nothing to do with me, nor has it anything to do with my intention

SERUMAGA Well talking about your intention, perhaps this is not really an intention, but how long do you feel you are going to go on with this choral poetry?

OKIGBO I don't know, I wish I could go on for ever, but as you see I don't write very often. In 1962 I wrote only one poem – the whole of 1962, only one poem – 'Lament of the Silent Sisters'. In 1963 I believe I wrote none. I probably wrote one or two things. But that doesn't mean that I don't keep working. Eventually I decide to present one or two. Last year I wrote 'Lament of the Drums' and 'Distances', but that was all. This year I wrote 'Painted Maidens' and 'Lament of the Masks',† and if tomorrow night for instance, I happen to write a poem, I write a poem; if I don't happen to write a poem, I don't bother. I do other things. Poetry is not an alternative to living. It is only one way of supplementing life and if I can live life in its fullness without writing at all, I don't care to write. I haven't got that type of ambition, which some people may have, of becoming a great writer or something like that. Because that is not an alternative to life itself.

* 'Lament of the Silent Sisters', published first in *Transition*; now included in *Labyrinths*, Okigbo's collected poetry published by Heinemann (AWS 62).
† Untraced.

Okot p'Bitek
BORN 1930

▼▼▼▼▼▼▼▼▼▼▼▼▼▼▼▼▼▼▼▼▼▼▼▼▼▼

Interviewed by Robert Serumaga in London in February 1967, Okot p'Bitek had published numerous articles in *Transition*, had written a number of works in Acholi and translated some, one of which appeared in 1966/67 as *Song of Lawino* (EAPH). The sequel, *Song of Ocol* (EAPH 1970) is planned as the middle section of a trilogy.

Other long poetic works by p'Bitek are due soon, one from a new publishing house in the U.S.A., Black Press, and *Song of the Malaika*, parts of which have appeared in the journal, *East Africa*.

SERUMAGA   Okot p'Bitek is a man of many and varied talents and interests. He came to Britain first in 1956 as a member of the Uganda football team which defeated the English Olympic team in 1956. When the team returned to Uganda, he stayed on and read Education at Bristol, Law at Aberystwyth University, Social Anthropology at Oxford, where he did his B.Litt. thesis in oral literature, and returning to Uganda he lectured at Makerere in social anthropology, organized a few festivals of culture, wrote a novel called *White Teeth* and a poem, *Song of Lawino*, and he's now returned to Oxford to present his thesis for D.Phil. in religion, and he's also Director of the Uganda National Theatre and Cultural Centre. Okot, how do you manage to do all these things?

P'BITEK   I think that there is always time for anything you like to do, anything you are interested in. I do not agree with people who say that they can only do one thing and you should be best at one thing only.

SERUMAGA   This book of yours, which is *Song of Lawino* a poem which has just come out and has got some very favourable reviews in the *Times Literary Supplement*,* for example, what does it deal with?

P'BITEK   It's a big laugh by this village girl called Lawino, laughing at modern man and modern woman in Uganda. She thinks that the educated folk are spoiled, in the sense that they don't belong, they don't enjoy fully the culture of the people of Uganda, and she thinks that if only these

* T.L.S., 16 February 1967, p. 125.

educated people could stop a little bit and look back into the village they would find a much richer life altogether.

SERUMAGA   After having been in Britain for seven years you returned to Uganda in 1963. Did you find that going back to the village sort of inspired you in the activities you were doing?

P'BITEK   When I was doing my work on the oral literature of the people of Northern Uganda, I first got the inspiration. I found that the poetry was rich, the oral literature was full-blooded, the dance was wonderful and the music just inspiring; and I just couldn't stop; I just wanted to go on and on, and this was the great inspiration behind the Gulu festival which has been going on for two years now.

SERUMAGA   Could you tell us more about the Gulu festival in Uganda?

P'BITEK   This is a festival of the arts, and as I said, it's been going on for two years. The first year it lasted four days, and last year it lasted seven days, and here we have all aspects of culture. We had dances, seven different types of dances, we had an art exhibition, children's play songs, a drama session, and a wonderful session on traditional games, games that people play in the villages, this was done in the countryside. We had a very successful art exhibition, which lasted only two days but was attended, or seen by about seven thousand people.

SERUMAGA   Gulu is in the north of Uganda, and the university at which you were lecturing, Makerere, is right in the south of Uganda.

P'BITEK   Two hundred miles.

SERUMAGA   How do you manage to combine these activities?

P'BITEK   Well, the university allow for field work to do research, and I was at that time helping in the extra-mural department. I had a tremendous time in Gulu, with a lot of people, educated folk who were very anxious to take part, and the great thing about this festival was that there were very few people coming just to watch, people came to take part, to take part in the dances and so on.

SERUMAGA   You mentioned the educated folk and of course you have these very scathing remarks about educated folk in your poem, 'Lawino'. What kind of participation was there from them, and what kind of educated young man, from the African *élite* took part in the activities you organized?

P'BITEK   We had Fellows of the Royal College of Surgeons, for instance, a Mr Odonga, who came from Malago for this week-end, and he was really completely involved in everything, carrying his tape-recorder with him, and taking part in occasional dances here and there: this is the sort of peak, the highest peak you can go, I think. And in the middle you had schoolteachers, bankers and everybody, it was a holiday and it was terrific. But in this book we have another category of educated folk. Those who really think that it's primitive to do these things without your shirt on and so on and so on, people who are over-dressed all the time, and so on.

SERUMAGA Do you find that these are the majority or are there only a few people in Uganda who are like that?

P'BITEK I think we had a large section of the educated people belonging to this group, but they are dwindling, I'm happy to say, because all over the place, in Kampala, whenever there is a party, you start off a traditional dance – any kind, Ganda dance, Ngoro dance, dance from the North – and everybody takes part in this and this is wonderful, and of course the band of the Uganda police and of the Uganda Army are playing these traditional tunes, and everybody is dancing; this is wonderful.

SERUMAGA Well, of course, dancing in the sort of Ugandan way, is not very different from the athletic exertions of the sportsman. Now do you still continue your sporting activities, apart from dancing?

P'BITEK No, not all, I play occasionally in games of football, I do a lot of running in the mornings, just to keep fit for the dances and so on, but I also think that in Kampala, especially among the big boys, there is much room for this athletic activity. There is a tendency to over-drink and over-eat, and, although they're very young – it's a youthful country as you very well know – at times you have a feeling that people are ageing quickly because they stand all the time with their brown files and so on, and then after that, whisky, and good food. I think we should have more athletic activities.

SERUMAGA In Uganda now you are Director of the Uganda National Theatre and Cultural Centre, and of course this is a very good position to sort of inspire cultural developments in Uganda, and there is the radio station which is very near where your theatre is situated, and of course the television station isn't very far away. Now, how do you hope to plan your activities so that you can integrate this into your development, and spread it wider into the country?

P'BITEK I think this is one of the greatest challenges I have ever faced, the Directorship of the national theatre, it's extremely exciting just to think about it. There is much room of course for working together with all the institutions you've mentioned, and of course you have more institutions to think of, the Department of Education for instance, to get involved in this. The major challenge I think is to find what might be Uganda's contribution to world culture. We're thinking of drama for instance: we should, I think, look into the village and see what the Ugandans – the proper Ugandans – not the people who have been to school, have read – and see what they do in the village, and see if we cannot find some root there, and build on this. And when we're thinking of music, the same thing, and poetry too. I think the people who are interested in culture, who have been to school, and to the universities, should become extremely humble and look to the people in the villages for inspiration and also for education. I think they have a lot to teach us.

SERUMAGA   Now this is a very interesting point, because when I was at school there was always a certain kind of furtive shame when one was placed face to face with one's culture. Some of us didn't have it but some did and I think this is probably due to some Christian mental processes that went into the African mind. Now you, lecturing in social anthropology in Makerere, and having done a thesis on religion in Africa for your D.Phil. at Oxford, how did you find the African students at Makerere university? How committed is the average student to his own culture, and how not-so-committed-to-it is he?

P'BITEK   I think there's no denying the influence of songs like 'Ba Ba Black Sheep have you any wool?' which we sang at Primary School, and the constant repetition by our teachers, mainly from England, that we must 'Progress!' We must change, we must have this new civilization; the fact that we learnt all about Shakespeare and so on has done something in our minds to make us, somehow ashamed, and at Makerere this is quite a major issue, because right through this educational meal they get this, and when they go to the university especially they begin to feel that they have had quite a big chunk of Western civilization and so on and it is this group which needs to be tackled very properly; and in fact some of *Song of Lawino* is directed to the students at Makerere in quite a big way.

SERUMAGA   I see. There is a theatre group, a travelling theatre at Makerere run by David Cook* how does your theatre hope to co-operate with them, to sort of bring together the two activities?

P'BITEK   We hope to work very closely together, if only because David Cook has done a tremendous service to theatre activity in Uganda. In the past he didn't have much help and co-operation from the theatre for one or two other reasons. I also hope that from the theatre side he will learn something more about producing things in the countryside and so on. Because although all through it was a great success, he hasn't had any proper criticism. For instance there were seven plays which were done in the vernacular, which were very good in some ways, but in many ways they could be improved, and in working together I think we will do a most wonderful job.

SERUMAGA   When I was talking to David Cook some months ago, he

* Now Professor of Literature at the University of Makerere, Kampala, editor of *Origin of East Africa* (H.E.B., A.W.S. No. 15, 1965) and with Miles Lee of *Short East African Plays* (H.E.B., A.W.S., No. 28, 1968).

and I agreed that in fact, the National Theatre in Uganda was nothing more than a very beautiful building, right in the middle of Kampala. Now do you agree with this, at the moment?

P'BITEK At the moment, I do. It's more than that, it's been used by one or two groups, in Kampala it's been hired by groups, it provides this facility. I wouldn't like to have a bomb on it or anything like this because it's beautiful, to start with, and the facilities there are wonderful and can be improved; now the main thing is to make use of it, and this is what I think we should be doing, to make full use of this place.

SERUMAGA There's a question which has been raised about theatrical activity in Uganda, which I don't think myself is very important but which needs answering. That is, that there are very few written plays in Uganda. How is your theatre going to cope with this situation?

P'BITEK Well this is quite true, we have one or two playwrights up and coming, but this doesn't worry me a bit, because I think there is so much in the countryside unwritten, a lot of myths and stories, folk-tales and so on which can easily be put on the stage. We have to do a bit of translation and I think there are quite a few people in Kampala now who are prepared to do this kind of thing. And what's more, we have a lot of plays, new plays in Africa which we need to experiment with. I am not against having plays from England, from other parts of the world, we should have this, but I'm very concerned that whatever we do should have a root, should have a basic starting point, and this should be Uganda, and then, of course, Africa, and then we can expand afterwards.

SERUMAGA Well, there is this idea which goes even further than that. Do you agree with the idea that the theatre in Uganda should not start from the National Theatre in the city and then spread outwards, but should start from the villages, and then build up to the National Theatre in the city, do you agree? How are you going to organize this?

P'BITEK I agree. I like to see the National Theatre as a kind of workshop, where we do a lot of experimental work. The problem really is that in the countryside we don't have artificial drama or artificial music, or anything like this, and by 'artificial' I mean things taken out of context. In the villages you have death-dances and marriage-dances and so on, and the poetry and the death-dances are about death, and they are very real, and when people are repeating these poems they are shedding tears at the same time. I would like to see that in the National Theatre we take this very real thing, very real drama from the countryside, experiment on it and see how we can project this. Not only from one part of Uganda to another because of the linguistic problems but also to the world.

SERUMAGA A question I would like to ask because what with my also being an economist and being involved in the theatre in some way, I find this a sort of worrying point. You are an educationist, a social anthropologist, a lawyer, and now you are a Director of the National Theatre in a sort of administrative sort of way. Do you find any conflict in your mind and your ambitions in these activities?

P'BITEK   No, I do not, in fact I find that with this kind of educational background I'm in a much better position to do justice to a very important thing which is the development of culture in Uganda. Of course, it's quite true that at this stage of our development in Uganda as in any other African country, we have very few people with the kind of education that you and I have had, and perhaps people would think that we should be better employed reconstructing the country – by this they mean building roads and so on, building trade and so on – but the cultural aspect of a country is equally important, in fact it's even more important than some roads, I think, and this means to me that we should also have our best men there in this field.

SERUMAGA   Well, of course this raises the question of the difficulty of the distribution of resources. Now the government, being bent on politics, and building roads and factories, how much help can you get from it financially, and, you know, morally, for the theatre?

P'BITEK   I think the Uganda government has been very good in this respect. They have, right from the foundation of the National Theatre, given a subsidy to the National Theatre. I do not quote the figures, but whatever they have given has been tremendous moral support; and recently a new ministry has been created, the Ministry of Culture, which shows, I think, this great concern by government in the cultural life of the country.

SERUMAGA   Yes, but of course creating a Ministry of Culture is one matter, and having the right man in it is quite a different case: Chinua Achebe's book *A Man of the People*, has a Minister of Culture in it! Now, is there the *right* attitude apparent resulting from the right sort of department being there?

P'BITEK   In the short time I've been in this job I haven't found any wrong attitudes, put it that way. I've found that the people in the Ministry have been helpful and are very, very anxious in fact to consult us on cultural matters and of course they are quite willing to entertain any ideas that are put forward, and where the money comes in they will do all they can to get what's required, but if they cannot get the necessary funds that's a different matter altogether. Another thing is that the constitution which set up the National Theatre has been changed in the last few months. In the past the Theatre only operated in Kampala, but now it's been expanded: we cannot operate outside, up country, which I think is a very healthy attitude on the part of the government.

SERUMAGA You're just about to return to Uganda, and I suppose that the National Theatre will take most of your time, but you are also a poet and a novelist, and I don't think you'll be practising law in the Ugandan High Court. Do you hope to continue writing poetry and novels, and perhaps plays?

P'BITEK Yes, indeed, I have up my sleeve quite a number of themes I'd like to do in the way of writing. I have to publish my two theses and this will take some time, but there are lots and lots of things I'd like to put into writing; it's not a question of time, it's a question of getting the right inspiration at the right time and then you just write.

SERUMAGA And of course from the point of view of organizing festivals, you couldn't be in a better position than now that you are Director of the Cultural Centre.

P'BITEK I would very much like to see this kind of festival, spread in other parts of Uganda, and of course to have a national one, for the whole country, in Kampala, in and around the National Centre. I think the world has a little to enjoy in Uganda in the way of culture, I think it's terrific and very rich indeed, and I feel very privileged to be in this position.

Richard Rive
BORN 1931

▼▼▼▼▼▼▼▼▼▼▼▼▼▼▼▼▼▼▼▼▼▼▼▼

Rive's interview with Lewis Nkosi was recorded in April 1963 in the first studios of Transcription Centre in Norfolk Street, London. Rive was then on the Farfield Scholarship which took him through East, Central and West Africa.

Short stories by Rive had been published in various South African magazines and newspapers and four of them were to form his contribution to *Quartet*, ed. Rive (Crown Publishers and Heinemann 1963). In the same year Seven Seas published a collection of Rive's short stories as *African Songs*. The next year his novel, *Emergency*, was published by Faber.

During 1964 he edited *Modern African Prose* (Heinemann).

NKOSI What, I want to ask you, is your comment on Ezekiel Mphahlele's analysis of the situation of writers in South Africa when he says that they find that they cannot work in the novelistic mode because the situation impinges so urgently upon them that they find that they have to say everything very quickly and they can only say this in the short story. Is this analysis true, or is it not?

RIVE Well, I would say it's true and it isn't true at the same time. It's one of those dangerous generalizations, I think, that have been very current in Africa that a certain mode of writing is the prerogative of a particular part of Africa decided very strongly by conditions appertaining there. Take the comparison, say, of South Africa and Nigeria, in which it is claimed that the short story functions in South Africa more prolifically for a variety of reasons and the novel seems to be the prerogative of Nigeria. Well, this whole theory I think has been thrown for a loop in that there are very, very many South Africans now – non-white South Africans – who are writing novels, contrary to this widely-held and often-expressed opinion. The reason put forward, that the moment of the situation in South Africa is so strong that it can only be captured through the medium of the short story, is true and untrue at the same time. What most people don't seem to appreciate is the fact that in South Africa there are levels and differences of oppression, the oppression is there certainly, but the degree to which it functions varies depending on the locality, depending very strongly on the geographical centre. Whereas I feel that it's wellnigh impossible for the writer to try and function as such in Johannesburg where things are very much sharper, he certainly has more of a chance of functioning in Cape Town where, for very many reasons, racial tensions are not quite as severe as up North. And this might explain why in Johannesburg most of the writers have either chosen voluntary or involuntary exile and the Cape has managed to retain its writers. In the Cape, writers were basically writing short stories not so much because of the situation impinging on them so very severely but that they felt that the short story mode was initially the best mode to get started and the discipline called for would stand them in very good stead when it came to novel writing.

NKOSI Richard, writing by white South Africans and black South Africans – what is it that distinguishes one from the other?

RIVE Almost nothing. I don't for one moment believe that there is a difference which is very obvious in writing which can be tempered by such surface manifestations as skin colour at all, and I don't believe in the point of view that certain writing in South Africa is the prerogative of and can be written only by a black man, or that certain writing in South Africa is the prerogative of and can only be written by a white as such. What is happening very strongly – and I'm very optimistic about this – is that a body of literature is emerging from South Africa which is going to be a South African literature regardless of the participants or the colour of their skins. At the moment, writing – well, not at the moment but up to now – writing has been virtually the monopoly of the whites in South Africa, and it has gone through different stages; gloating colonialism, passive receptacles, liberal mouthings, sweet – completely dripping wet – with certain very sickly sentimentalities, but now that we have a writing emerging in which we have participants from all so-called racial groups, a synthesis is arriving whereby I feel, personally, I am writing as a South African, not as a non-white South African or a white South African, and I certainly believe that any progressive writing in South Africa from whites would most probably take the same road. An example of that, for argument's sake, would be *Episode* by Harry Bloom,* a book for which I don't hold a particularly strong brief, but which I feel does portray the black man as an active participant in what is happening, not as a passive receptacle.

NKOSI Yes, James Baldwin started off by saying that he wasn't a negro writer, that he was merely a writer. And he has moved full circle to a position in which he finds himself now, writing as a spokesman of the

*Republished as *Transvaal Episode* by Seven Seas Books (1959).

negroes but trying to transcend the position in which he finds himself ethnologically put in. I was just wondering about you, Richard, whether you see yourself as just a writer or do you find yourself located within a certain ethnic group and do you see yourself as part of that group?

RIVE   I certainly do not see myself as part of an ethnic group and I certainly do not see myself as a spokesman for a particular group as such. I've read the same book of Baldwin's and I was very interested in his point of view: you remember he says that as an American coming to Paris he found – he felt very strongly his Americanism, and I think of one rather brilliant essay on Richard Wright – I think it's called 'Poor Old Richard' – he speaks about Richard Wright's inability to Africanize himself on his rather ill-fated venture into West Africa. Well, I feel the very same way, too. I feel that my experience is a culmination and a synthesis of all experience, regardless of where it came from. I'm not going to do what the negritudiners do – and, by the way, negritude I think is a completely false and ridiculous philosophy which should have been exploded years ago instead of now coming to the forefront. I feel that the good work produced, the poetry of Senghor and others produced in this particular phase is good not *because* of, but *in spite* of, this rather ridiculous back to the womb, literary – anachronistic kind of philosophy. I feel that, as I've said before, if a writer writes out of his experience he's going to write about things which directly affect him which he feels, which he appreciates. And I am nothing other than a South African and I felt South Africanism very strongly once I started travelling. I have been through Africa, and in the places where I have been to, the interesting thing was that I felt as foreign there, in spite of my colour, as I felt in Italy or Greece or anywhere else. I did feel that this was not a sense of belonging at all. I couldn't function as a writer in these countries, the whole situation was completely different: I am not an Ethiopian, I am not a Ugandan, I belong to the southernmost tip of the Cape Province and from there I function, I am urban South African, and I do not wish to be anything else.

In May 1966, when Robert Serumaga interviewed Richard Rive in the Dover Street Studios of Transcription Centre, Rive was on his way back to South Africa after a year's studying in the United States.

SERUMAGA   Richard, you were born in Cape Town in 1931. Can you tell me a little about your early life in Cape Town?

RIVE Yes, I was born and I lived for a fair portion of my life in Cape Town's District Six, which is a coloured slum area and which forms the geographical location not only for my writing but for the writing of quite a few other coloured South Africans – people like James Matthews* and Alex La Guma and so on.

SERUMAGA There is a bit in your story 'The Strike' which reads as follows: 'His face was dark brown with heavy, bushy eyebrows, and a firm jaw. His hair was black and wavy. In Durban he could pass for an Indian, only his accent gave him away.' Richard, is this you?

RIVE Well, this is not the first time I've been asked this question, not only in this particular story but in others. Yes it's me and no it isn't. I think like most other writers, my writing does tend to be autobiographical so there is more than a fair share of myself in a lot of what I say. But essentially Boston in this story is like most of my other characters and that is a combination and a synthesis of many people and many attitudes. The superficial description there might fit in, I think, although I'm not quite so sure.

SERUMAGA Now let's get to Boston's thinking, superficially he might look like you but let's see if you differ from him in your thinking. Now he has an argument with Lennie, which reads as follows: 'The strike leader, says, "What a way to welcome the new republic." Boston accelerated his pace. "You are helping to distribute leaflets tonight." "No." "Why the hell not?" Boston turned on him, "I'm a painter not a pseudo politician." "We're all in on this." "Are we? I've not been invited." "That's not funny at all." "Didn't intend it as such." "Must you go through life as a cynic?" "If you prefer it that way." "Oh go to hell." Boston always felt annoyed at Lennie when the conversation reached that stage. It had happened often before. He knew it was useless to continue in the same strain. He would start arguing and the more excited he became the more cynically Lennie would react. Finally it would sink to the level of personalities. He walked on moodily refusing to continue the conversation. "Cigarette?" Lennie asked. "Peace-offering?" "Come off it." "No thanks." "Oh well, artists of the world unite." "Your world is so small." "I love it." "Comfortable, isn't it?" Boston sneered. "Very, but it doesn't cramp my style." "Ah, but your style is extremely limited, isn't it?" "Terribly so, confined to posterity." What price arrogance? They continued their silent walk.'

* Born Cape Town, 1929 – published in *Pan African Short Stories* (ed. Neville Denny; Nelson, 1965), Komey & Mphahlele's *Modern African Stories* (Faber & Faber, London, 1964 and 1966) and in Rive's own *Modern African Prose* (A.W.S. No. 9, 1964) and *Quartet* (A.W.S. No. 14, 1965). Also in various magazines.

Now, Richard, what is your side, is it Boston or Lennie? Are you committed to a philosophic cause as a writer?

RIVE Well, you asked me two questions. Now the first question: 'Am I Boston or am I the other character?' I mean: Are my ideas like those of the characters? Again yes and no. On the whole I let the characters speak for themselves, and I try and follow the argument myself. I couldn't quite say I agree with either the one or the other, or that I completely disagree with either. Now, this might sound very vague to you, but it's the dialectic. It's the framework of the dialogue in my writing that I find terribly exciting, because for once I'm in a position whereby my characters can make statements, which I need not substantiate. This is the way they think as individuals, although I presume that I have some manœuvrability, but so far and no further.

My idea of the writer within the social context, this is going to sound like a truism but we have to say this so often because people so often miss the point and cloud the issue: we are a synthesis of all our experience, arising out of this, his particular experience, the writer is going to create so that much of what he does will be autobiographical. Very many of the views expressed will be his, and certainly I feel that the writer, to a certain extent, is an interpreter of the society in which he finds himself. Sometimes he happens to be a Cassandra, but that's unfortunate. So that I think it's going to be the death of the writer if he's going to completely restrict himself and limit himself to think along the line of particular party politics. What he does with his private life is his affair but if he, in his writing is going to do that, he's going to skate very, very near the thin edge of outright propaganda. In which case he's a writer too, but can he lay claim to being a creative writer? You see I'm not decrying the polemicist but it's not quite the same field.

SERUMAGA Now in the stories I have read which you have written, you seem to be very much engaged with the colour problem in South Africa. Admittedly this is a very big problem, and it must colour almost all issues. But do you think it limits you, or does it sort of inspire you to write?

RIVE It does both. There is this limiting factor, limiting from the point of view that the issue itself, although it is a universal one – I came across this in America and very many other places as well – still tends to the parochial in terms of the South African situation. Now, I do not presume you must go to the other extreme, and in the middle of what is happening in the Republic of South Africa write about a boy falling in love with a girl in the Protectorate of Basutoland; if you want to do that it's your business. But a writer as I've said before, cannot help being an interpreter of the synthesis of his individual experience and in terms of that is going to write about things which directly affect him, and in South Africa he can never escape the colour issue.

I may say though that I haven't been doing serious writing for some time now, and it's most unlikely that I'll – in fact its a truism that I won't be able to – write the way I did before – but I think with a certain amount of maturity and so on my theme won't be such outright protest as it was before – not that I'm decrying the outright protest that I felt before. I feel it's a very necessary situation to go through, but with this breaking out of that, you're throwing off some of the limitations of outright protest, and you start to see issues in their wider perspective. That is why I don't really feel, think and feel that I would ever write like this again.

SERUMAGA In another story which you wrote, 'Resurrection', there's this family which is mixed, some of the children being white or appearing to be white and others not. Now there are these distinctions in South Africa between the blacks, the coloureds and the whites. Where would you define yourself as falling?

RIVE Now that's an invidious question. Racially I have been defined in South Africa as coloured, whether I except it is another matter. As a bit of light relief: an American negro asked me down south whether 'you are one of those coloureds you spell with a "u"?' so presumably I'm one of those coloureds you spell with a 'u'.

SERUMAGA Now does this affect your life to any significant extent, I mean apart from being generally non-white, but being coloured as apart from black?

RIVE Well, yes. Look I think I can quote somebody, I'm not quite sure what the reference is, 'I was satisfied with being black, until I discovered I was non-white', because this has all sorts of connotations implicit in it. And in South Africa certainly yes, legally, socially, and so on, I am affected by being a member of a particular racial group as opposed to being a member of another racial group.

SERUMAGA In this story 'Resurrection' you seem to be deeply religious, at least your characters seem to be. Now, I'd like to ask you, when you say 'Shall we know Him when he comes', what is your belief in God in this respect?

RIVE I'm afraid you're asking all the most invidious questions, and for the first time I think I'll have to put down my religious views on tape. No, I'm not deeply religious – unfortunately, or fortunately, as the case may be. I've gone through all the fashionable phases which every bright young undergraduate goes through you know, agnosticism, theism, atheism, etc., and I'm very, very confused from that point of view at the moment. I'm not sure, as the Americans say, whether God is dead or not. What I do know as an artist is that religion intrudes very often in what I write. Maybe this sounds somewhat pedantic of me to say, but I almost feel the way, say Wordsworth or Hardy or Lawrence felt: that it's not an orthodox religion which he's interested in, but something much wider in it's ramifications which he's trying to explain not only to the readership but to himself. And I'm also through this writing bit trying to explain a lot of things to myself which I'm still unsure about.

SERUMAGA Now you've spoken about being an undergraduate, which university did you go to?

RIVE Ah well, that was metaphorical. But, I'm a graduate of the University of Cape Town, and I'm a graduate of Columbia University in America.

SERUMAGA What did you do after you graduated from Cape Town?

RIVE I taught, English and Latin, and I wrote; I did a lot of writing after that. Then I was awarded a Farfield Foundation Fellowship Grant which gave me time to do research and travel very widely through Africa and Europe, visiting most countries in the two continents. I went back for another spell of writing and teaching, and then I was given a Fulbright Grant which took me to Columbia where I did a Master of Arts degree in English Literature.

SERUMAGA What do you think of America where you've just been, and where you went?

RIVE It's a great country – I went with all sorts of misgivings because, you know, I'd read the right books, and I formed stereotypes and a lot of my views remained the same and very many of them changed. But on the whole I found that Americans were wonderful people. It took a long time – I was very aggressive in my outlook when I went. I'm re-reading with very great interest now Pepper Clark's *America Their America*,* because he too went to America, and I met him immediately after he came back but I had not been for such a length of time, and I read the book for the first time before I went to America, and it's very interesting reading it now.

SERUMAGA Don't you agree then with J. P. Clark in his book about America?

RIVE I think that one's experiences depend on where you go, the social group in which you move, the attitude of people towards you and, of course, your own particular attitude. I certainly have nothing to complain about. What I would say is that his experiences were very different from mine. He went to Princeton; I went to Columbia. He might have found

* See Clark's interview with Andrew Salkey, pp. 71–74.

the social circle in Princeton not very compatible; I found the one in Columbia very conducive to pleasant recollection.

SERUMAGA What was your relationship to the negroes in America, was it as you expected, or was it different?

RIVE No, it was different, and it was the same. They had a lot in common and they had a lot of things which were different. I feel that at certain basic levels the situation in America is analogous to the one in South Africa and at very, very many levels it is not analogous. I certainly didn't find so many points of contact whereby I could say this is an emotional experience with which I could identify myself, I mean basically identify myself with any form of repression, anywhere, whether in America or otherwise.

SERUMAGA Would you care to name some of these levels, that were identical and not identical?

RIVE Well it's not identical in terms of the negro's position as a minority group; in terms of legal acts of desegregation in America; in terms of the American negro's attempt to identify himself within the mainstream of American culture or in terms of that rejection, looking towards Africa, or in terms of that rejection looking towards the history in the South. It's all an attempt to find himself and to define himself within the status of a society which by and large still rejects him, whereas at no time did, or does South African society, or *could* it, possibly, reject three-quarters of its population (I mean the whole thing is completely ridiculous!); whereas American society can fairly successfully do that. There are very honest attempts to de-segregate, and there are very, very dishonest attempts to maintain the *status quo*.

SERUMAGA Now what has been your occupation while in America?

RIVE What work did I do? I did a Master's Degree at Columbia University. I worked under Professor Robert Bone on American Negro Literature; my especial field was the Harlem Renaissance, which was a kind of outburst almost, of literary activity in Harlem, during the 1930s, which produced people like Ralph Ellison, Richard Wright, Langston Hughes, Arna Bontemps and all the people who are really almost legends now in American literature. Then I was very lucky too because I did very much of my research at Langston Hughes's home and got a lot of invaluable help from him, and through him was able to spend some time with Arna Bontemps, who, I think, apart from Langston, is the only survivor of this particular period.

SERUMAGA Now, it seems this situation is very much in contrast with what you found in East Africa. You did say, in one of your books, an anthology, that writing from East Africa was very scarce. Has anything happened since you wrote that sentence to make you change your mind?

RIVE Oh yes, I would have changed my mind right there. I felt when I was in East Africa that the writing there was exciting by potentiality. Unfortunately, there were very few people really creating, but once you have people like Ngugi,* for instance, who is a prolific writer and I feel a good writer as well in addition, this must set the pace for a lot of activity happening there. Oh I'm more than prepared to repudiate – not really repudiate that because at the time I was there this certainly was the situation appertaining, and it certainly isn't the situation now. I don't think so much has come, they're not really seriously competing yet, West Africa and South Africa, but it's just a matter of time before that is so.

SERUMAGA Who, among the African writers first, and among other writers do you think you like most?

RIVE Well, I think we'd better restrict it to African writers, because among other writers I have so many people from Chaucer upwards. But the African writers – you know the unfortunate thing about being a writer yourself is that you know so many people as individuals, and this does cloud your judgement somewhat. But in West Africa certainly I like Chinua Achebe† very much; Wole Soyinka,‡ of course, is miles ahead of very, very many playwrights, not only in Africa but throughout the world – he's really a great playwright; I like Pepper Clark's§ work very much. In South Africa itself the situation is becoming somewhat critical because most of the really good writers have left the country, and are either in voluntary or involuntary exile, and very few are still remaining; and how much potentiality there is within the framework of that I'm not sure. But they certainly have produced one or two very good poets like Adam Small‖ who is a coloured poet in Cape Town and produces really good work – in spite of or maybe because of the situation in which he finds himself. Zeke Mphahlele,¶ of course, is still the grand man – and I say this very respectfully – the grand man of African literature; he's done an enormous amount for it. Unfortunately, you see, we are dogged by very many factors like differences in yardsticks, differences in measurement, success coming too soon so that very many of us become smart-Alecs, and we feel that we write well before we ever *start* creating. In spite of one or two critics who claim that

* See pp. 121–131.
† See pp. 3–17.
‡ pp. 169–180.
§ Cf. pp. 63–74.
‖ Writes chiefly in Afrikaans. Represented in Jack Cope and Uys Krige's *Penguin Book of South African Verse*.
¶ See pp. 95–112.

people like myself aren't over-modest I think we do realize our limitations, but we also realize not only our potentiality, but our ability to spread that potentiality in terms of African literature. We are at the beginning of so many things. Most of us are first generation educated people and even in terms of my background I don't think anybody in my family has ever gone as far in formal education as myself so that there are a lot of factors against which we are pitted.

SERUMAGA What do you plan to do when you get back?

RIVE Go on teaching I think, and go on writing.

SERUMAGA What subjects do you teach?

RIVE Well it sounds a bit like murder. I teach English literature and Latin and I kind of specialize in dead languages, not that English literature is a dead language, but I taught Anglo-Saxon and Latin and things like that.

Wole Soyinka
BORN 1935

▼▼▼▼▼▼▼▼▼▼▼▼▼▼▼▼▼▼▼▼▼▼▼▼▼▼▼▼▼

This interview made by Ezekiel Mphahlele was recorded in London in May 1962.
During the preceding two years Soyinka had done, among 'quite a number of other things', research into African drama. Much of his own drama was already known; much of it performed. None of his work had yet been published.
The flow was to begin in 1963: *Three Plays* (Mbari 1963), *Five Plays*, (O.U.P. 1964; *The Swamp Dwellers*, *The Trials of Brother Jero*, and *The Strong Breed* of *Three Plays* and the two later ones). Then *The Lion and the Jewel* (O.U.P. 1963), and *A Dance of the Forests* (O.U.P. 1963).
In 1965 *The Road* was published (O.U.P.) and in the same year Soyinka's only novel thus far, *The Interpreters* (André Deutsch and Heinemann 1969).
Kongi's Harvest (O.U.P.) appeared in 1967, as did his collection of poems *Idanre* (Methuen). Other poems have appeared in numerous anthologies and a small group of two *Poems From Prison* (Rex Collings 1969) was published in pamphlet form. A recent play of Soyinka's and two early radio plays have been produced but not yet published.

MPHAHLELE   What is usually the relationship between the performer and the audience in indigenous Nigerian theatre?

SOYINKA   One of communal participation. There is very often, as always with these things, a strong exhibitionist impulse, you know, motivation, which really is the beginning of what you might call 'conscious-performer-to-audience' theatre, as we understand it. There is a great deal of that. But I would say that of the bulk of say, the religious ceremonies, for instance, are things for entire communal participation.

MPHAHLELE   What about entertainment purposes?

SOYINKA   For entertainment purposes? Well, you have the masquerades, you know. The masquerade element is really a lot of entertainment. Some of it, of course, has a very deep, religious significance very often, but you will find that, especially with the Yorubas, the masquerades are really, you know, dressed. They are really dressed up theatrically for an audience.

MPHAHLELE   How do you see this idiom – this traditional idiom in African theatre being worked into the pattern of modern theatre?

SOYINKA   As far as I am concerned, it is an inevitable step because it is – it is a kind of material with which one is confronted practically every day – well, it may not be so much in the towns, but at least the atmosphere of it persists, even as it is carried over maybe in the songs in folk-lore. These are things which dramatists – an African dramatist, or, even more important, a producer, would find immensely useful. I will say producer in particular because, as I said, these are theatrical idioms. And for the producer, you know, these are priceless because they will inject novelty – a freshness into his interpretation. They might lead, in fact, to a theatrical revolution, the moment African writers and producers become very conscious of the potentialities of these idioms.

MPHAHLELE   In your own work as a playwright, to what extent do you try to reconcile these idioms?

SOYINKA   Well, as a playwright, you notice that I make this distinction in a producer-playwright. I produce as well, you know, and so very often in writing the play, for instance, I try to interpret a modern theme, using one of the idioms of dance or mime. In a play like *A Dance of the Forests*, for instance, I tried to use a lot of the rites, a number of religious rites and – there's one of exorcism, for instance, which I tried to use to interpret a theme which is quite completely remote from the source of its particular idiom, because of...

MPHAHLELE   Ah yes. That's right. The open air theatre, which is part of the Mbari writers' and artists' club in Ibadan: are you using this for the purpose of experimentation?

SOYINKA   Yes. But Mbari theatre, we have found, is really a killer, a play killer. You cannot do a lot because of continuous background noise, you know: taxis, radiograms blaring. It is terrible, but we have produced two plays there recently. Oh it was terrible, from the point of view of audience, too distracting. But what we are trying to do is to encourage all sorts of theatre companies to come and rehearse there or have their try-outs there.

MPHAHLELE   And probably you can even have try-outs in front of a limited audience.

SOYINKA   Oh yes. We brought this Duro Ladipo.* He is one of these

---

* Born in Oshogbo, Western Nigeria; *Three Yoruba Plays* (translated and adapted by Ulli Beier, Mbari Publications, 1964); 'Moremi' (in *Three Nigerian Plays*, ed. Beier, Longmans, 1967).

Yoruba folk-opera writers and producers and he has come to perform there quite a few times before audiences.

MPHAHLELE How do you see this whole thing that we have been talking about influencing your radio play production?

SOYINKA Well, I can only give a personal example of that – a play which was commissioned two years ago for independence by the N.B.C. – *Camwood on the Leaves*, in fact, this is in print right now. What I tried to do in this play was to utilize the idiom of the masquerades in auditory terms and I think it worked.

MPHAHLELE That's interesting. Since you wrote *A Dance of the Forests*, have you written any other plays?

SOYINKA Yes. Mainly one-act plays. *The Trials of Brother Jero* and *The Strong Breed* – oh, this is another play in which I have used these African ceremonies where the town is cleansed on the New Year – where you have a sort of carrier. You might have noticed some masquerades, well, they're not masks as such, but they are painted either half red, half white, or else all black and they are called 'akogun' and this really emanates from the purification ritual. These people go through the town and the real meaning – the significance of it is that they sort of take away a lot of evils from the town. Well, I have used this idiom in this play *The Strong Breed*, whereby a man, the hero of the play, if you like, the main character, finds himself in this position where he is sort of hounded to death, almost sacrificed just for the purification of a town. I find in fact that these things crop up inevitably.

MPHAHLELE Always – yes. Yet, I am not aware of any work that has been written on African drama – traditional drama as we have been talking about.

Soyinka has not yet been able to publish a systematic and integrated study of the material gathered from his research.

The pressures on his time then and since are partially indicated by the fact that this interview following was recorded by Lewis Nkosi with Soyinka in Lagos, August 1962.

NKOSI Well, Wole Soyinka, could you tell us what set you off on this road to writing?

SOYINKA I suppose that requires really going back a bit. I would say I began writing seriously, or rather taking myself seriously, taking my *writing* seriously about three, four years ago, but I can only presume that I have always been interested in writing. In school I wrote the usual little sketches for production, the occasional verse, you know, the short story, etc., and I think about 1951 I had the great excitement, of having a short story of mine broadcast on the Nigerian Broadcasting Service and that was sort of my first public performance.

NKOSI   What schools did you attend?

SOYINKA   I went to Government School, Ibadan; after that I spent a couple of years in the University College, Ibadan.

NKOSI   You have now published drama or rather you've had some plays produced?

SOYINKA   Yes, 'produced' is the correct word. I haven't had any plays published although some are in print right now and will come out shortly.

NKOSI   Could you tell us what those plays are?

SOYINKA   There is *The Lion and the Jewel* which was the first play I wrote.

NKOSI   No, the second.

SOYINKA   The first one I sent up, I suppose like most people do, is the *A Dance of the Forests* which I wrote in 1960 and timed it for the Independence Celebrations; there is the *House of Banigeji* which has never been performed. And I have written about four one-acts including *The Trials of Brother Jero* which was done quite recently in Nigeria.

NKOSI   The *A Dance of the Forests* won you a prize, didn't it?

SOYINKA   Yes, Nigerian Independence competition prize 1960.

NKOSI   Have you got any particular authors that have influenced you most?

SOYINKA   This is a very difficult question for me because I am not aware of any conscious influence on my work, but I can say that if I wanted to aim at any particular kind of theatre, I think, however subconsciously, I might aim at Brecht's kind of theatre which I admire tremendously, just his complete freedom with the medium of the theatre.

NKOSI   In your last play, *A Dance of the Forests*, which caused a lot of people a tremendous amount of agony trying to figure out just exactly what it was trying to do – they felt that there were some hidden meanings contained in lots of symbolism which they couldn't gather. Now as you're the author, we are lucky to have you here and, we think that you probably might enlighten us about just what you were trying to say in that work of yours.

SOYINKA   Well, let me say first of all that I think that my prime duty as a playwright is to provide excellent theatre, in other words, I think that I have only one commitment to the public, and that is to my audience and that is to make sure they do not leave the theatre bored. I don't believe that I have any obligation to enlighten, to instruct, to teach: I don't possess that sense of duty or didacticism – very much unlike Brecht for instance, for, you see, what I like in Brecht is his sort of theatre, it's liveliness and freedom, not so much his purpose or intentions. I believe my primary duty is just to see that I provide excellent theatre for the audience. But inevitably, it is just common sense to say that one just cannot write about just nothing. In *A Dance of the Forests*, I was very much conscious of all the potentialities of existing theatrical idioms in Nigeria and I only know that there was one thing which motivated, may be, guided the form and the shape of the play or the eventual fate of the characters. I use this word 'motivated' quite cautiously because I do not think I consciously tried to preach or bring out, you know, a series of symbolisms at all, but the main thing was the realization that human beings are just destructive all over the world. I think this is it – I have thought about this again and again but during the production – I produced it myself – and in trying to see the play take shape on the stage, I find that the main thing is my own personal conviction or observation that human beings are simply cannibals all over the world so that their main preoccupation seems to be eating up one another. This I think is the main thing I would say was in the back of my mind when I wrote it.

NKOSI Yes, that sounds very much like Tennesee Williams's idea of the world conscious of the evil.

SOYINKA Well, I don't sort of regard it so much as . . .

NKOSI The ferocity of human beings.

SOYINKA Yes, the carnivorous nature of . . . .

NKOSI Yes, I wonder whether now – have you pursued this theme in the other plays or are the other plays different?

SOYINKA . . . Fundamentally, I think they're different. I think that sort of semi-consciously the moment I realize I'm pursuing a theme again, it seems to ring a bell warning that I have preceded myself somewhere; I have such a feeling about this that I shirk from it but I would say there are traces of it in my other plays, in for instance, my favourite one-act play which is *The Strong Breed*. I think this one is also very much mixed up with the whole element of sacrifice, so contrasting the idea of selfishness with willing self-sacrifice as opposed to the other general cannibalism of human beings.

But I would say that, faintly, it is present in other plays, but I don't allow it to – you know. . . .

NKOSI   Yes. Well, pursuing this idea further, it would seem to me that you are diametrically opposed to, say – the writings of French West Africans who seem to assume that the profound generosity possessed in very large measure by the African people stands in contrast to other peoples of the world.

SOYINKA   Yes, I know what you mean and I agree with you entirely. In fact I think that one of the most humbling discoveries any African can make is just the fact that he can actually interpret the greed and, you know, the general evil of – what you call the European world in the faces of his own personal and intimate companions. I think that after years of self-delusion, a very chastening discovery – I should say rediscovery, because one lives with this all the time – the chastening rediscovery is to find that – and it's a terrible knowledge – that given the chance and the circumstances your best friends are capable of . . . I think this really is why I'm opposed to this idea of singling out one's own race as being a leaven of the . . .

NKOSI   Yes. It is the same kind of idea contained in the story in the Bible about the publican who stands there in the open and says, 'I thank thee Lord, for I am not as these other men are!'

SOYINKA   Precisely, and it just is not so.

NKOSI   Wole, tell me, which one of your works did you find most difficult to shape and to work on?

SOYINKA   I find it's the comedies, quite frankly. I just can't describe to you how absolutely delighted I was to find that I had written *The Trials of Brother Jero* which in production and in reading I find people enjoy tremendously. This is a comedy, a very light recital of human evils and foibles. I found that *The Trials of Brother Jero*, and *The Lion and the Jewel* were, in fact, quite frankly, like most comedy in the theatre, the most difficult things to write.

NKOSI   Well, this is interesting, because it would appear to lots of people who've followed especially your poetry – I've just seen a poem reproduced in *The Times Literary Supplement* – it would seem, reading that poem, that you have a very natural gift for comedy or satire.

SOYINKA   Yes, I suppose satire especially, as opposed to sort of a more . . . no, no, no, I mustn't say that. No, I think satire requires, to begin with, a very strong feeling about something and I think why 'Telephone Conversation' – which seems to be the favourite of anthologies, quotations, everywhere – why it appeals to people is that it really implies, it has this undercurrent of very strong feeling but one overcomes this and tries to see the humorous side of it. I have noticed this, in fact, the very same thing with the 'Immigrant' poems which I hate now and which I want to forget, but which I'm not allowed to forget! But generally I find people take to these much more easily.

NKOSI   What are you working on at the moment?

SOYINKA   Let me see. Well, this is an accurate statement. Well, let me ... I'm working on another play.

NKOSI   Well, are you working on a novel, anything like that, I mean you have been working on plays and poems, and people seem to think that you might just venture into another form, something different like a novel. Have you ever considered ...

SOYINKA   Well, I'll be quite frank about this, I'm writing a novel and it's nearly finished, in fact, and should be published early next year.

NKOSI   Would you like to say anything more about the novel?

SOYINKA   I think really this is where my feeling of a sort of personal-relationship cannibalism comes pretty much to the fore: in the novel. In fact, that's the main thing I can say about it.

NKOSI   That's very interesting. At the Mbari Artists' and Writers' Club in Ibadan, this school of writers or it may be inaccurate to call it a school, but there's a group of young writers who seem to be very much in contact with each other and with each other's works; have you known these people long, and who are they?

SOYINKA   Well, there is Christopher Okigbo* whose poems are going to be published very shortly by Mbari. He is a very, is a highly gifted poet, very musical poet I find and enormously influenced – this I do not like particularly this side of him – influenced by Ezra Pound, T. S. Eliot; it shows too much I think in his work. There's J. P. Clark† who wrote this very successful Grecian tragedy, *Song of a Goat*, which we performed at Ibadan. There are poets like Gabriel Okara,‡ J. P. Clark, of course also writes poetry. We have painters like Demas Nwoko,§ who is also incidentally interested in theatrical designs, he has just spent a year in Paris and I think he did one or two designs for some operas. He's coming back now, so I think over the next year there's going to be some collaboration and some quite exciting work. . . . There are – let me see now – there's Uche Okeke,‖ who is a painter as well. We exhibited him not so long ago at Mbari. Chinua Achebe,¶ of course, the novelist; he is not very active at the Mbari

* Cf. pp. 133–147.
† Cf. pp. 63–74.
‡ Author of *The Voice* (H.E.B., A.W.S. No. 68), poems in *Modern Poetry from Africa*, eds. G. Moore and U. Beier (Penguin, 1963) and a bigger selection of poems in Howard Sergeant's *Poetry from Africa* (Pergamon, 1967).
§ See *Black Orpheus*, No. 15.
‖ Drawings of whose were published by Mbari, 1963.
¶ Cf. pp. 3–17.

for the simple reason that he is in Lagos, so we don't see much of him really.

NKOSI   But tell me, do these young people sort of approve each other. What kind of life do they live?

SOYINKA   Approve – not at all! I mean this is what I like about Mbari, quite frankly. There is no attempt to evolve a kind of representative, shall we say, trend in Nigerian writing: it's a group of individuals amongst whom presumably there mightn't even be more than two people who give a damn for each other's work, but the important thing is to have a centre to which people are brought, who are just interested in what the central core are doing and who can meet and drink and, you know, just get on with their work and collaborate whenever it is possible with such diversified talents.

NKOSI   What do you feel is the greatest lack in Nigeria at the moment as far as your life as a writer is concerned, or otherwise?

SOYINKA   The greatest lack I think quite frankly is criticism. We have not at the moment got good critics in Nigeria and European foreign critics are not helping by being Eurocentrically condescending, applying a different standard for writing. I think they're always astonished that anything can come out of Africa at all, and this makes for, you know, a great deal of over-estimation of our own potentialities in Nigeria. I remember I got rather sore about this once and I arranged what we called a writers' palaver in which the idea was to confront writers with critics, and just have a free for all, you know, a real slangy session. Unfortunately, the few critics who do appear, even when they, let's say they, praise the work or when they damn a piece of work, don't know what they're talking about at all. They damn it for the wrong reasons, most unintelligent; so we invited newspaper critics, reviewers over the radio, people who'd introduced books on television, and this first one was not as lively as it was expected to be: it was too much weighted on one side. Anyhow, we are going to have some more like that, and I have no doubt we might be able to build up a really fearless but very honest and intelligent critical form.

NKOSI   Yes, or if you might link that with the problem of audience. Now, what do you feel your audience is in Nigeria?

SOYINKA   Well, I find that the audience in Nigeria are very, very accommodating in this sense: they're really curious and this is why criticism is so important because, you know, a critic's job is not merely to review an existing piece of work but also to create an atmosphere of appreciation, of tolerance; to cultivate an experimental attitude not only in writers but in the audience, and you do find, to go back to this play, for instance, if I may use my own personal example, *A Dance of the Forests*, which most people said, as you know, they could not understand; well, the people who claimed to understand it had different versions of its meaning. But what I found personally gratifying and what I considered the validity of my work, was that the so-called illiterate group of the community, the stewards, the drivers – the really uneducated non-academic world – they were coming to see the show every night, and they used to come backstage and ask if they could come in without paying, because they never had the money to pay for it. If you allowed them, they always felt the thing through all the way, and they came night after night and enjoyed it tremendously. I never asked them what they made of it, you know. The important thing is that there was something in it, enough to make them want to see it again, and I think this is true of most of the Nigerian audience. The only time when they become quite frankly lazy is when they find that their instincts to reject what seems strange are supported by a columnist in the paper, then they suddenly feel, 'Oh! yes, we thought that you know, I mean what's all this nonsense', but left to themselves, and given the proper guidance, I have no doubt at all that we have one of the most interested audiences, in any event, in any cultural event, here in Nigeria.

NKOSI What do you personally conceive of as your audience? Are you writing for Nigerians or writing for the world?

SOYINKA This may be an unrealistic thing to say, but quite frankly, I do not think of any audience when I write. I write in the firm belief that there must be at least a hall full of people who are sort of on the same wavelength as mine from every stratum of society and there must be at least a thousand people who are able to feel the same way as I do about something. So when I write, I write in the absolute confidence that it must have an audience; but production is a different thing. I will adapt, I will alter any play in production for the particular audience I am working for. I have to take this into consideration. But in the actual writing, I don't think I need bother my head, or anybody need bother their heads at all about the audience, whether Nigerian or the European.

NKOSI To put one further question, possibly the last, what do you think is your future? What are your plans for your future?

SOYINKA It's simply this – that the sooner we can get a professional theatre going, the better. I would like to be able to work full-time in the theatre. I find I'm as much interested in producing and in acting as I am in writing and with a professional theatre, I find I can live a very fulfilled existence.

The third interview with Soyinka was made by Dennis Duerden in London, in August 1965, during the time of the Commonwealth Arts Festival.

DUERDEN   Wole, your recent production of *Kongi's Harvest* in Lagos was made with two companies, the Orisun theatre and the 1960 Masks, so that you had half your actors from Lagos and half from Ibadan, in fact they were living about ninety miles apart, didn't this make for some special difficulties in mounting this production?

SOYINKA   In fact I can answer that question in a few words. We will never do it again. Mind you I said that also about two years ago which was the last time any such production was undertaken, what we call a two-city production, but this particular play required actors from both sides and I just found that to obtain the kind of standard I wanted I had to go back to this old method of production, which we thought we'd seen the last of. But you're right, it caused a lot of difficulty, in fact the production expenses amounted to fifty per cent being taken up by the transportation alone.

DUERDEN   But are you going to do *Kongi's Harvest* again when you get back? Which company are you going to use this time?

SOYINKA   The same company. Well, there'll only be one or two revisions, I mean we're not going to rehearse for as long a time as we did before, with practically the same production.

DUERDEN   Where?

SOYINKA   We will do it both in Lagos and Ibadan.

DUERDEN   One of the things I noticed was that you were acting as the producer, the director, the stage designer, and finally on the last night you were doing the lighting as well, I think this was a great feat, but didn't you find it a bit of a strain?

SOYINKA   Once again, I just say what I always say after every experience like that, never again, but well the situation of theatre in Nigeria is such that you find yourself in this kind of predicament with a most distressing and monotonous regularity. You begin the production with all the responsibilities neatly mapped out and with a number of people being enthusiastic about it but what happens is, the designer suddenly finds he has to go off somewhere to hold an exhibition, the lighting man is transferred to some out of the way place, the movement director maybe has got a sick grandmother and he's got to go there, and in the end you know, it's the same old story again.

DUERDEN   Ideally, I suppose, you would like simply to direct your plays and to have all the production and all the other worries taken off your shoulders?

SOYINKA Ideally I'd just like to sit down and dictate my requirements. Yes.

DUERDEN Wole, this play is mostly about the theme of an African dictator, when you produced it in Lagos with a Yoruba setting, would you say that this play could be adapted to apply to African dictators generally?

SOYINKA Yes, as I explained in the programme, I was very anxious that the fact that I used a Yoruba background, that this should not be taken to mean that it is referring specifically to some Yoruba dictator, of which there is none by the way at the moment, although I know at least half a dozen would-be dictators in Nigeria, but you're right it's meant to apply to the whole situation, the whole trend towards dictatorship, on all sorts of spurious excuses, in the newly independent states in Africa.

DUERDEN I thought actually that it could in fact be produced with English actors, or with American actors, that what it said about dictatorship could be extended outside the frontiers of Africa.

SOYINKA Yes, as a matter of fact I was telling somebody that my ideal organizing secretary would be an American actor seen in similar roles.

DUERDEN Now the first part of the play was a conflict between your African dictator 'Kongi' and a Yoruba Oba, and in your second part of the play the Oba had really given place to his son, so that the conflict was between the dictator and the Oba's son, and the play seemed partly to be about the way in which the Oba's son took over the role of opposition to this dictator. Would you say that this was a general comment on the situation of young people in Africa today?

SOYINKA I would say it's true of the part of the Oba himself, true in this sense, that the Oba's were not equipped to fight this new kind of dictatorship and one by one the traditional institutions fell before the onslaught of these new power-rapacious national leaders. You will find that where there has been any constructive and realistic resistance it has had to come from the younger generation. So in a way this is a historical observation, but I do not want you to understand this as meaning that I am optimistic about the younger generation, because I find that they seem to succumb more easily to the prospect of sharing in this power, of making sure they are on the right side, rather than taking the risks involved in opposition.

DUERDEN The young man who was playing the part of the Oba's son, Dapo Adelugba, has now come to London to play a very different role, at the Theatre Royal, Stratford, the role of Murano in *The Road*. He must be a very adaptable young actor to play these two roles. How do you think he'll cope?

SOYINKA Well Dapo is very versatile, as a matter of fact he was originally supposed to play a very different role from Murano when I discussed it with the director, originally he was to play Samson, but of course he couldn't come here early enough, and he had to begin rehearsals so somebody else is playing that. I don't think Dapo will find any difficulty at all in coping with this.

DUERDEN Judging from the performance I saw in Lagos, neither do I, thank you very much, Wole.

Efua Sutherland
BORN 1924

▼▼▼▼▼▼▼▼▼▼▼▼▼▼▼▼▼▼▼▼▼▼▼▼▼▼▼

When Maxine Lautré interviewed her in Accra in April 1968, Efua Sutherland had stories published in anthologies, for instance, 'New Life at Kyerefaso' had appeared in Rive's *Modern African Prose* (Heinemann, 1964).
The following were in book form: *The Roadmakers* (Ghana Information Service 1961); *Playtime in Africa* (New York, Atheneum 1962). The plays, 'Foruwa' and 'Edufa' were in *Okyeame* Vol. II, No. 1 (1964) and III, 1 (1966) respectively, as well as another, 'Ana Segoro' in *Présence Africaine* XXII, 50 (1964).
The two plays from *Okyeame* were to become available in book form as *Foriwa* (Ghana State Publishing Corporation 1967) and *Edufa* (Longman 1967), and *Vulture! Vulture!* with *Tahinta* appeared as two (illustrated) rhythm plays with some music (Ghana Publishing House 1968).

LAUTRE   Efua Sutherland, I have heard it said by somebody that you are the pivot around which all the drama in Accra circulates.

SUTHERLAND   Oh! My goodness.

LAUTRE   It seems you are terribly busy because you are managing about four plays at the Drama Studio and at the Writers' Workshop organizing poetry readings and editing *Okyeame* and running experimental village theatre so I don't know how you find time at all.

SUTHERLAND   There is no difference really between my work and my fun and I get a lot of fun from this. I do things I really want to do which I suppose is one of the most fabulous things anybody can say about their existence. I had wanted to live in this way, you know, and somehow it's happened, I'm thrilled, so I can put out the energy; I seem to be able to put it out. I somehow get the energy to do it. I suppose it is a sense of joy that I have in doing it that keeps me going.

LAUTRE   Can you tell me about all the facets of drama that are coming together now, Efua?

SUTHERLAND   Yes, I've just done a little paper which I will give you, which is called 'The Second Face' – a review of the theatre movement in Ghana. I reckon that with the setting up of an Arts Council of Ghana in 1956, a very conscious step was taken towards encouraging the development of the arts here, and 1956 is over a decade now and during this time, you know people's images and interests have been canalized into all kinds of things. From the Arts Council's own point of view, they have tried to encourage little drama groups all over the place, both in Accra and in the distant regions. They have set up arts centres in this period of time all over the place and sometimes groups of people have come from the country to Accra to perform. They have Arts Council representatives at these centres doing work in the regions now and encouraging the painters and little drama groups and so forth. So in a wider sense, you know, this kind of thing is going on all over the country but the focus of the movement has been in Accra, I think, where somebody like myself for example has gone forward and set up a Drama Studio, which is conceived as a centre for very vigorous experimentation in drama. It is conceived as eventually being a formative process in developing writers and so forth. I have had, the Drama Studio has really come as another expression of my desire to have more and more people involved in writing because I started a Writers' Society before I built the Drama Studio to get more people interested in the business. Primarily of writing for children, I must say, but later on it turned out, that not everybody is interested in writing for children, there were people, lots of people, who were interested in writing. I felt that to give another reason why people would want to write I would build the Studio and develop the experimental theatre programme for people interested in writing them.

LAUTRE   And what exactly happens at the experimental theatre?

SUTHERLAND   I would like to tell you – before I tell you in detail about that, I would like to tell what other people have been doing, you know. I told you what the Arts Council has done on a countrywide basis and what individuals have done and I have just mentioned as a start on that what I tried to do. But, you know, there have been other people like Philip Behoe who is employed by the Arts Council but whose special interest is music. He is very anxious to have a national orchestra in Ghana – he is the man who wrote the National Anthem, Philip Behoe. So he has been trying with that over a period of years and now he does have a group which is giving public performances. I am sure he would like; there are all sorts of needs, of course, that have come as a result of these various programmes – I'm sure Philip would welcome some foreign aid – a European orchestra that is really trying to teach us, you know.

LAUTRE   Yes, but it's Ghanaian music.

SUTHERLAND No it's music.
LAUTRE Just music.
SUTHERLAND It's music. It's not jazz, it's classical music that he is involved with, and there is Vincent Akwete Kofi, who is a sculptor, you know him don't you?
LAUTRE I've heard of him.
SUTHERLAND Yes. He represents, you know, a wave of rather fascinating sculptors like Oku Ampofu. There was Kofi Amtubam, of course, who died. Painting is represented by a group called the Akwapim Six who are located in the Eastern Region.
LAUTRE They have had exhibitions at the Arts Centre?
SUTHERLAND Yes, and at the Central Library; and so forth. Art exhibitions are becoming more of a feature, you know, in the movement.
LAUTRE I see there's an art contest here at the moment, isn't it being sponsored by Mobil Oil or something?
SUTHERLAND I think so. Yes that's quite a new thing for a business organization in the country to sponsor an art exhibition and I think it's one of the processes of this development that this has happened, you know. In the painting, I'm not so convinced that the painting here is very exciting yet, you know. There are individuals like Kofi Amtubam again whose work is of course known on a world basis.
LAUTRE And Bucknor?
SUTHERLAND Well Bucknor is post-Kofi Amtubam. I think Kofi Amtubam was Ghana's most eminent painter, you know, there's Bucknor now and there's another man, and this is the man whose work fascinates me most, you know. I find something there. This man is Bartimeus. He is one of the Arts Council organizers posted in the Eastern Region at Koforiua and if you have the chance you should by all means look at some of his work. There's a young painter now – the College of Technology has a painting department – the Department of Fine Arts and some young painters are coming out of there. There's one young man who graduated last year for example who has gone on to the Slade and returned only recently, and he's determined not to go back into teaching. This is a new thing – not to go back and take a job but to exist on his own as a painter, you know. It rather reminds me of Ama Ata Aidoo who has done this in the writing field, you see.
LAUTRE You think he will be able to make it?
SUTHERLAND He is a very determined young man and he has just painted the mural on the bar scene for *Everyman* for me, you will see it tonight. A strange painting which shouldn't be in a church I'm sure but it's there. So you see, there's a movement – I feel this. Groups, individuals,

and so on. I've talked about the individuals in painting. You've met Joe de Graft, have you? ...

LAUTRE Yes.

SUTHERLAND Who was connected with the Drama Studio and we are both connected with the School of Drama up in Legon which in itself is an outcome of the Drama Studio programme.

LAUTRE Didn't they have it before?

SUTHERLAND No. The Studio was first, in fact some of the first students of the School of Drama in Legon were people that passed their apprenticeship at the Drama School.

LAUTRE Really?

SUTHERLAND Yes. It's a natural development. The school is a natural development from the Studio programme. When we were doing the Studio programme one of the frustrations was since we were using people who were not full-time, you know, we could have a six-man hard work with a group and then some people get transferred from Accra or all sorts of things could happen and we couldn't keep a group together. Also we had problems to do with performances. Sometimes we'd be performing and somebody would be on night duty, you see, so it was very necessary for there to be a programme which was concerned with training full-time people.

LAUTRE People couldn't be transferred away.

SUTHERLAND That's right, full-time people. So we have that now, people who have been through the school and are available. Unfortunately the country is not ready to absorb them yet – not directly into theatre. But this will happen. It will happen.

LAUTRE Do you find the audience response encouraging?

SUTHERLAND Oh well, there's a lot to say about that and with audiences as with the experiments themselves, you know, you can see the processes of development. You can see audiences seeing plays which they are hard put to relate with, for example, the language problem – Ghanaians. I maintain that it is in theatre that we are discovering what a foreign language English is, because our productions in English have a long way to go to achieve standards you know, just because we don't wear the language comfortably you see. I am doing an experiment now with this experimental group of mine, the production – our first production – is in Akan and this is a very deliberate choice, you know. There is no comparison between their capacity to communicate in this language and what they do in English, but I am hoping that this company is eventually going to be bilingual.

LAUTRE Which company is that?

SUTHERLAND The Kusum. Yes that's the company doing *Everyman*, and I was telling you about the School of Drama – Joe de Graft and I moved from the Studio up to the school. We have been joined by other people, in fact we ought really never to talk about separate schools of Drama but of the School of Music and Drama which I hope will eventually become an idea – a fixed idea that there's a School of Music, Dance and Drama, you know. Joe has written some plays, I have written some plays, there are other young people who are coming up who have written plays, Ama Ata has written plays. There is a young boy for example – he's talented, but he has come through the School of Drama, his name is Martin Owusu, he has written a play which I think will be published.

LAUTRE Tell me some more about what you're doing at Atwia – your experimental village.

SUTHERLAND That's another aspect of this thing. You see I am very anxious for the things we are doing to have meaning in our society.

LAUTRE Communicate a message?

SUTHERLAND Not a message but to be able to communicate. You don't always have to have a message when you communicate. You are thinking through a problem or something. If this is a problem which forms the theme of your play you ought to be able to communicate it. It's simple – the aim is that Ghanaians shall understand the art that we think we are doing you see – that's all. It's as simple as that. I find that with the state of development of Ghanaian society in general – as in fact of all societies in Africa – there've been all sorts of problems – there are all sorts of confusions which God knows everybody's analysing, but then somebody can counter that with, 'But there's confusion all over the world.' But I think we have very particular things to do in evolving culturally.

LAUTRE What sort of things?

SUTHERLAND Well, one is to free ourselves from the confusions of trying to project our personalities through foreign media. We can't do it – it sits very ill with us I find. Language is one of them. I think that there will come a time when English will become a Ghanaian language. I'm pushing in the interest of this objective – that English becomes a Ghanaian language and not a foreign language – I'm pushing with the objective of a bilingual society in my mind in some of the things I do. So for example you see in my work, in my writing, I write for children and now you see that some of my works are in both English and say, Akan, which is my language.

LAUTRE In the same play?

SUTHERLAND No, these two versions of the same play; an English version and a Ghanaian language version. I am anxious that children are started off bilingually in the schools.

LAUTRE   Yes, is that happening?

SUTHERLAND   No it won't happen for some time, and it can't happen unless there's literature in support of it. So this is all part of my experimental programme. Find out what can be translated in both languages towards this end.

LAUTRE   So the children in Atwia are absorbing much more than elsewhere. They're developed to be able to understand, I mean, more of what you are doing?

SUTHERLAND   I am there with them. They are not conscious of what my preoccupations are, you know.

LAUTRE   But what, the way they respond to your plays, you would like in future all the children, all the children to be able to.

SUTHERLAND   Yes, I would like in the future for the children to be able to express themselves as well in English as they do now in their vernaculars, in their mother tongue. That's the objective of the children. I said some of the things we have to do for our cultural evolution ... there's a lot of experience, historical experience which has shaped attitudes and opinions in the society.

LAUTRE   You mean the traditional ...

SUTHERLAND   Not traditional. For example the slave trade happened to us, didn't it? We were participators in this – there is a residue of experience from this historical fact, and if you look at oral literature for example you will find that oral literature has coped with it – the experience. It uses this experience artistically. Now I don't see us doing this in English for example and I am anxious for us to remember that people were not born this morning – a society was not made this morning. A society has been formed, you know, by circumstances of history, etc., etc.

LAUTRE   Like colonialism?

SUTHERLAND   Colonialism is another of the facts of history, and their attitudes to it – for example you look at ordinary communication today in any town in Ghana, in any home, and you find attitudes about white people. These are being communicated daily between person and person naturally. There are all of these things ready to use. So I would prefer us looking at it and using it – or myself and a few other people – to just doing imitative art like just performing plays just because they exist in books already. You see what I mean. They're there always to be used by anybody, but we have a duty to create some.

LAUTRE   Yes, well, how do you mean imitative, because creative isn't imitative is it?

SUTHERLAND   Maybe I was using imitative quite consciously not to mean creative. So it's an exciting thing – there are all sorts of exciting things to venture and I take a deep breath and venture forth – not that one is sure what one is doing. I'm on a journey of discovery. I'm discovering my own people. For example when I went to school – I didn't grow up in rural Ghana – I grew up in Cape Coast with a Christian family and all. It's a fine family and all, but there are certain hidden areas of Ghanaians like – and important areas of Ghanaian life, which I just wasn't in touch with. In the past four or five years I've just made a very concentrated effort to make it untrue that I do not know my people and I know them now.

LAUTRE   Do you find that coming out in your plays? Are they developing?

SUTHERLAND   Oh yes, very much so.

LAUTRE   What are they about? Your recent one – I see you've done one on Ananse.

SUTHERLAND   Oh yes, this is going to the mines next week-end to play to mineworkers in a diamond mine.

LAUTRE   And *Tweedledum and Tweedledee*?

SUTHERLAND   Is a children's play. You see I work at these various levels. *Tweedledum and Tweedledee* which is just a lark. I like Lewis Carroll, and the children are reading *Alice in Wonderland* and *Through the Looking Glass* at school but finding it terribly difficult, so I thought that I would give them a means of enjoying it. So *Tweedledum and Tweedledee* is just a fun play thrown in for the fun of it. But *Ananse and the Dwarf Brigade* is of the other kind – it's a play developed from folk-tale for children. It's going with *Tweedledum and Tweedledee* as a pair. It's developed from folk-tale with a very conscious piece in there and poetry of the countryside to turn the children's attention to the thrills they are in touch with, really, in their play and so on, but which I don't see exploited in the books that they read at school.

LAUTRE   Do you feel that the University, I mean for instance, the School of Drama, is helping the general acceptance of African literature looking towards . . .

SUTHERLAND   There is a movement now for African studies in all universities, I think, in Africa. And at Legon there's an Institute of African Studies which is doing a lot of work in African literature. I think that the students, all Legon students have to do some African literature now. It is inevitable that work in African literature and this kind of thing increases with the years now. The School of Drama – there is a School of Drama and a School of Music, you have seen these haven't you? Have you met Bertie Opoku? He is in charge of the dance end of the School of Drama, and there's Dr Amu, that fine gentleman, who is in charge of music and you've met Professor Nketia who is in charge of it all? I think that when the school evolve and it is in the process of doing so now, it's only three or four years, and that's not time enough, but when the school has found its part – it hasn't found it yet – I don't think when it has found its parts I am sure, it's going to be a very important link to this whole movement and it would really be wonderful then to have a complex of programmes geared towards a theatre movement. At the school you'd have the training – general training programme, up there at the school. The Studio was conceived as an experimental centre and this is going to be for all time necessary. If the Studio manages in the next two or three years to develop a company, a resident company idea, which takes in really talented people after the school course, to do a professional apprenticeship before they pass on to professional companies eventually all over the country – that's what the Studio can do and that links up with the school. And then the Arts Centre, if it establishes regional theatres.

LAUTRE That's what it's trying to do?

SUTHERLAND Yes, I think so. I think this is what it has to do now, you know, in fact it is rather urgent for the Arts Centre to concentrate on this kind of development now – establishing the regions strongly, so that the personnel being trained now can be absorbed all over the country.

LAUTRE So that they can pass from one to another?

SUTHERLAND Yes. Some people talk of a National Theatre building and there's an incredible confusion of terms, around here, but I think that people first, that playwrights and companies first – the country doesn't have much money. It should spend this money on people and the establishment of real first-rate organizations, and then learn what to build. And meanwhile I see nothing going on for which there isn't a place already existing for them to perform.

LAUTRE There seem to be quite a few places!

SUTHERLAND I have been completely awed by what is called the 'concert party' organization in Ghana – the concert parties are drama troupes – they are mobile drama troupes.

LAUTRE Nothing to do with the Trios?

SUTHERLAND The Trios is an old name for them and they have a fabulous organization. In fact this is the only – first professional theatre in Ghana. Yes. Last vacation this was one of my special areas of study, the concert party.

LAUTRE It's very popular, isn't it?

SUTHERLAND Oh my goodness, yes! Ghanaians accepted this art completely.

LAUTRE But, it's not new anyway, is it?

SUTHERLAND   Oh no! It started way back in, I think it was the early thirties. There were these Trios.

LAUTRE   A bit similar to the Nigerian folk opera too, isn't it, in that it hasn't got scripts. It's fairly spontaneous, full of movement.

SUTHERLAND   And music and dance. So it's going to, that's the theatre that has been accepted, you see, and the new things we are trying to do. I think literary drama has a long struggle to go. I hope it doesn't succeed too quickly – even though I'm writing. I think that communication is what must be aimed for and we must learn what kind of art to do by listening to the people, feeling with them, being very sensitive about this society.

LAUTRE   And developing from that, from more straight, less movement lines, slowly . . .

SUTHERLAND   It will be slow. Evolution takes it's time in spite of what we would like to happen.

LAUTRE   Anyway it's very fascinating, and how do you find time to do everything?

SUTHERLAND   I do, that's all. I like doing it and that's all there is to be said I think. It's also quite wonderful to see as you go on this journey of discovery how you measure up in your society.

LAUTRE   I don't think you've done too badly.

SUTHERLAND   It's very revealing. Educated Africans should, particularly if they say they're going to be artists, I think they should go through this test.

LAUTRE   They must be in touch?

SUTHERLAND   Go through this, go and hear what the people think about them – the ideas are just hilarious.

LAUTRE   How did something like *The Lost Fisherman* go down?

SUTHERLAND   I saw *The Lost Fisherman* when it was done in Ga, but I haven't seen the English version. I liked it when I saw it in Ga, I haven't seen the English version yet, but I suppose I will.

LAUTRE   There seem to be so many things happening – George Wilson and the Drama Studio and the Arts Centre, and the International Drama League, it's almost impossible to work it out from a distance, what's happening.

SUTHERLAND   I think that's one of the healthy signs of the movement going on because the ideal thing seems to be for a great many groups to experiment, nobody has the answer to how to do theatre for this society yet – not by any means, and so I like this incredible explosion. Everybody is trying to find an answer and eventually the audiences will tell us.

LAUTRE   Yes, I'm sure they will.

SUTHERLAND Eventually they will tell us. In Accra you can easily get the kind of audience which gets into a car at eight-thirty and drive to The Studio – to the Arts Centre, to the Community Centre – this is good, it's all right.

LAUTRE Are there that many of them?

SUTHERLAND Oh yes. I mean, you can have a show packed by that kind of audience. But then this is not all there is in audiences, and some people should try for other types of audiences. What about all those thousands of people in Accra who do go and see the concert parties? You know the concert parties? Last year I first saw the circuit begin in a place outside of Accra – I saw it near Tema in a little sort of caravan post – it's a settlement, it's an outcrop of Tema and they were doing it in a cinema. I arrived and the company was there and I said, 'My goodness, they have a hope!' But the show was packed. One cedi flat. So there is an audience of at least 500 workers.

LAUTRE That's quite a lot, isn't it, to pay, at least?

SUTHERLAND For that place. Whoever they are, these people are willing to put down their ten shillings and see a show. So that's there. If we stay in Accra and just cater to an eight-thirty drive-in audience, we are not doing our job.

LAUTRE Yes.

SUTHERLAND So trying for different kinds of audiences and I think some of the different groups that are going now can cover quite a wide span of audiences and this is a very good thing.

LAUTRE Yes, I was just thinking how it relates to London, for one feels that all the audiences there are the sort of high-falutin ones. I suppose for musicals and things there are other audiences, but I suppose they aren't very artistic half the time.

SUTHERLAND Well, we can't afford to start off not artistically, we can't afford that. You've had a long history of the growth of the theatre in England. There's no comparison. If we are starting out on this thing we had better start with art hadn't we? I have been trying to guess from the present situation what some of the hopes for the future are. I think we will get more writers. There are signs of a lot more interest, for example, in writing plays, a lot more interest in writing literature in general than seven years ago, even five years ago.

LAUTRE Because people can see their work? Yes?

SUTHERLAND Yes, there are avenues through which their work will show, you see. I can see connected with that the development of indigenous publishing. All of it is related, you see. That makes me very happy. And I hope that a lot more people will write for children. I hope so. There are not enough yet at all. But there's a lot of work waiting for them. Sometimes I've heard people talking – I haven't engaged in the dialogue on African literature, I have kept my mouth shut. But I've heard people discussing at conferences the role of the writer – all this rigmarole, well, if there's any role, they should write for children.

LAUTRE Well it's going to be the next lot of people.

SUTHERLAND That's one of the most important roles I can think of, you see. First of all they've got to expose themselves to African opinion, that's one thing, and secondly, I think one of the roles is to write for children. The country through it's Government-sponsored agency which is the Arts Council, can't afford the expense of really what this development involves – can't afford it yet. I think it would be wrong for writers, for artists to get into the habit of depending on given aid of this sort, also I think it does the writer no good because it makes him lazy.

LAUTRE And he won't be so subject to public opinion then, will he?

SUTHERLAND That's right. But I feel for the writer of stories or the novelist there is a market. A young man here, Asare Konadu, is demonstrating the need for this kind of writing for a general readership not for school market. His novels are not the highest grade in literary writing by any means, but he is publishing here and he is selling out in editions of 15,000 or more, so I think the future of that is very good indeed. It's been demonstrated.

LAUTRE Because you do need a body of literature even if it is not of a terribly high standard, just to make comparison and to build up the whole thing.

SUTHERLAND That's right. That's hope for the writers of the future.

LAUTRE Does he publish through the State Publishing Corporation.

SUTHERLAND It's his own publishing house. He staked on himself and it paid off but now he is publishing other writers, for example we have passed him the writers of the national programme. He has just done a book *The Secret of Opokua* which is a children's novelette written by a lecturer in classics at the University of Ghana.

LAUTRE They had an extract from that in *Okyeame* was that right?

SUTHERLAND Yes.

LAUTRE It was very nice.

SUTHERLAND So that is – there is a widening hope, vista of hope for the writer. Then I think theatre should go all out and get self-supporting. There are these audiences I'm talking about. I sat through shows with a thousand people who have paid down their money – just the ordinary general run of Ghanaians who've paid their money and are prepared to sit through a four-hour performance.

LAUTRE Concert parties?

SUTHERLAND Now we should look at that very carefully and if we can, get that audience too. If we can get that audience too, if we can, we will get them.

LAUTRE I think it's quite urgent to try and get them as early as possible so that they are diversified into . . .

SUTHERLAND We will get them if we make a big push on this company idea. I'm taking a big risk at the moment in trying to create one – the Kussum Company, and it's a very big risk. I tell you I'm not nervous – I'm not nervous at all.

LAUTRE But that isn't so far away from the concert party, is it, really? Or is it?

SUTHERLAND Well in its practise, in its material, it is. But in its practise, we've moved the company out of the studio to go out to all the audiences, and they are going to travel more and more until I hope somebody will give us a travelling theatre kit so this will aid us to do the job faster.

LAUTRE That sounds like the right idea.

SUTHERLAND To do that faster, I'm trying to discover a method of company. It's a piece of research in itself. How do you do it? I have brought for example, a little girl from the Trans-Volta settlement – the New Volta Settlement, whom I heard singing on one research trip – leading a local girls' band of singers beautifully. Now that was three years ago, but when I thought of Kussum (she has a very special aura to her), I went back and I got her, and now although I cannot pay her a salary yet, and she needs a probation, what I'm doing for her is to maintain her – give her maintenance allowance until she has trained and so forth. As she is there, there is a young man who has had some secondary education and has gone as high as he can – can't go any further, he's going to be a very good stage manager – he's just going to be terrific, so this month because we are making a little money now, I'm going to be able to take him on. He has been working with us for nothing.

LAUTRE Really? Is he stage manager already?

SUTHERLAND Not yet. He has been helping the stage manager, and he has been extremely good.

LAUTRE What is his name?

SUTHERLAND Victor. I would like Victor to train in lighting and sound and here is another area where help would be welcome. I've welcomed some visiting people who come here for example to work for the company for short periods, even six weeks, a month.

LAUTRE Do you find . . .

SUTHERLAND Oh yes, he has been. He has just come of course and he is taking the trouble to survey the field and to assess where he can best put his talent, you know . . .

LAUTRE Is that the sort of person you want?

SUTHERLAND Oh yes.

LAUTRE And what's the girl's name?

SUTHERLAND Afi, Afi Abefi, that's her name. There is another girl, she is a very talented actress. This girl is called Ablei Nguabi, you will see her in the bar scene tonight at the show. She is a very talented person. She didn't have much education but as part of her programme of training within the company, she is being taught by somebody who is a teacher in the company, to advance her general education. She is getting lessons for the advancement of her general education apart from her training in theatre. That's how I'm making the programme that I have – the individual training programme and the company training programme. Well it is very fascinating really.